# The Joy of Growing Older

## by Peter Mustric

Tyndale House
Publishers, Inc.
Wheaton, Illinois

Library of Congress
Catalog Card Number
78-68913. ISBN
0-8423-1974-3, paper.
Copyright © 1979 by
Peter Mustric. All rights
reserved. First printing,
August 1979. Printed in
the United States of
America.

# CONTENTS

# FOREWORD

Senior citizens are the most neglected and misunderstood group in the average church. For three decades, the church has put a priority on young people, youth pastors, ministers of evangelism, Christian counselors, and business managers. But very few churches have ministers particularly called of God to pastor senior citizens. Consequently, very few churches have an effective ministry to senior citizens within their church, much less an evangelistic outreach to those in their community.

Dr. Peter Mustric was led to take the position of Senior Citizen's Pastor in our congregation three years ago and has clearly evidenced the fact that this was a call from God. For the first time, we have a regular program that ministers not only to the many that can attend meetings, but to those confined to home through disabilities. He even uses senior citizens to reach senior citizens in a most effective manner.

*The Joy of Growing Older* covers many of the unique insights he has on the needs of these people. In fact, I found it extremely beneficial in my relationship with my own mother who had just retired and moved to San Diego. As I read the book, I realized one of my mistakes in dealing with her and it has been extremely helpful to see her situation with his insights. They have given me a whole new appreciation for her lifestyle. Consequently, it has simplified the decision-making process.

I can confidently recommend this book not only to retired persons but to their children. By writing it, Dr. Mustric has done a great service to the church and to the Christian community in general.

Tim LaHaye, Pastor
Scott Memorial Baptist Church
El Cajon, California

# INTRODUCTION
## WHEN ONE RETIRES

During a recent trip to the Midwest, I was almost besieged by middle-aged people in their forties and fifties who wanted to speak with me concerning their aged parents, in-laws, or grandparents. Because of longer life spans, the problem of aging is becoming a major topic of conversation and for some a serious dilemma. Just what is causing this wholesale concern on the part of well-adjusted Christian children?

I certainly don't profess to have all of the answers. But as Minister to Senior Citizens at Scott Memorial Baptist Church in San Diego, and as one who has enjoyed twenty years of experience in the ministry and a number of years in practice as an optometrist, I do feel that I can shed some light upon the issues involved. The situation may be labeled "gigantic" because it eventually will involve the bulk of our 22.9 million senior citizens in America as well as their loved ones and friends.

In our church, we minister to more than 600 people over sixty years of age and thus encounter firsthand many of the difficulties which the elderly face day after day. In addition, because we live in a town with many Navy retirees who leave the service relatively early in life, we often confront a compounding of retirement and age problems. People used to die before seventy years of age. Now many live into their eighties and even nineties, and this presents a new series of problems for everyone.

Christian children who love their parents and in-laws, and see them slipping, want to be helpful and supportive. Sometimes they overract in order to show their concern. The main problems are emotional. Financial problems arise occasionally, but these are usually due to emergencies. When serious financial problems exist, they have generally been present for a number of years and surface during retirement because of other problems. How to supply retired elderly parents with emotional and spiritual support as well as occasional financial advice and help when needed is a concern of prime importance. This book will endeavor to show how to do this, as well as to outline some important goals for young people so that they might avoid the pitfalls that come along later in life.

Fifteen years ago, nursing homes admitted men at age seventy-three and women at seventy-four. Now they are admitting men at age eighty-three and women at eighty-four. The aged seldom return home when they enter at this age. Thus their families are faced with the financial, emotional, and spiritual problems, as well as the physical plight, of the elderly.

How these problems are handled very often determines the family's well-being and unity. A satisfied, relatively happy parent in turn contributes to a content and secure, rather than a guilt-ridden, family. This book endeavors to aid children and the aged alike in seeking solutions to some of these problems and frustrations before they arise and in analyzing them within a biblical framework.

# ONE
# GROWING OLD GRACEFULLY/
# THE GENERAL PROBLEM OF AGING

Someone once said, "We are born to die." Indeed, after the first ten to twelve years of life our bodies begin to do just that, though mentally we continue to grow and expand. Too often in our haste to put Aunt Jane and Uncle Jim in their graves because they are slowing down, we forget that *their minds* may still be youthful and creative.

Despite age and its attendant problems, some of the greatest contributions to society have been made by the elderly, the so-called "old fogies." From Moses, the great law-giver of the Old Testament, whose natural strength was unabated at 120 years of age; and Abraham, who sired Isaac at ninety-nine years of age; to the Apostle John, who gave us 1, 2, and 3 John, and Revelation at over ninety years of age, God's chosen leaders have frequently been senior citizens. Even in secular fields we find the same thing holds true. Gladstone wrote some of his best works in his sixties and seventies. Franklin was a great diplomat in his seventies, and Stokowski and Rubinstein performed brilliantly at over ninety. Bismarck, Lloyd George, Winston Churchill, Clemenceau, General MacArthur, and a host of others were also creative and active right into their eighties and nineties.

Recently one of our seventy-five-year-old "Live Wires" said to me, "I don't feel any different than I did at forty." Obviously he didn't mean that he could run as fast, jump as high, or do as many pushups as a middle-aged man. Nor was he suggesting that he was a stranger to aches and pains. He was simply asserting that his mind was clear and sharp (and it is) and that on good days, the years didn't really seem to matter at all.

Actually, an elderly Christian with all of his faculties is no different inside than you or me, strange as that may seem. The eighty-year-old wonders I know are people whose *bodies* have simply gotten older and who have developed a different set of problems and needs. They are often spiritually stronger than ever, indefatigable workers in the church, and very much concerned with the spiritual values and lives of their loved ones and friends.

Why, then, do elderly people act in ways that tend to drive their children up the wall with worry? Why do they ignore their children's advice, drive alone at night, keep too much cash at home, and handle their own bank accounts? It's often because they are concerned with two basic problems—*self-preservation* and *security* with personal autonomy. They simply want to retain their standard of living and their way of life and dignity to the end without being a burden on anyone. What's wrong with that?

Most of their children who counsel with me are concerned about their parents living alone. They worry that their parents will fall and hurt themselves or face illness alone. Some are also anxious about their parents' financial resources. Yet I have found few children regularly send their parents a small check to help each month without being prompted or pushed into it. If there is a financial problem, isn't this a logical way for well-heeled children to respond? By contrast, it is usually the parents with limited resources who are sending checks out of their poverty to offspring in their fifties and sixties! Not always because the offspring need it, but because they complain of their imagined needs in letters or in person. This seems to be a particular sin of our generation in spite of our many blessings.

However, the majority of those with whom I counsel really want to do what is best for their parents—as long as it does not cost them too much—so that the elderly can enjoy their retirement years. When we begin to realize that, barring senility or a stroke or some debilitating disease, our aged parents are fully capable of thinking and acting, once they have all the facts, we begin to appreciate Law #1 of the aged: *Leave them alone if they are reasonably happy, well-adjusted, and able to take care of themselves.* You can't make them happier by running their lives or by uprooting them and forcing them into your life style. It just doesn't work!

Law #2: *If their present habitat pleases them, don't uproot them without an extremely good reason to do so, or you will live to regret it.*

Law #3: *If they can handle their money and property, don't try to take this pleasure away from them.* After all, they've earned it. Let them keep a sense of security and occupy their time managing their estate.

Law #4: *Take them into your confidence and let them know you're around and willing to help if they have need.*

Law #5 continues in this vein: *Ask for their advice and use their expertise.* It cost them a lifetime to get it, but you can have some of it free and make them feel good in the process.

Law #6 urges in conclusion: *Don't try to force your opinions or life style on them.* In most cases they are happy with their own.

Uncle Harry worked hard all of his life, saved his money, owned his own home, and lacked nothing. As he grew older, his only relative, a nephew who lived nearby and was his conservator, became upset because the roof leaked, the house needed painting and airing out, and Uncle Harry didn't always wear clean clothes. Yet Uncle Harry was happy and secure in his little house. "What should John do?" asked John's wife, who really loved Uncle Harry. My response to her was, "Keep on inviting Uncle Harry over for occasional meals, continue to take Uncle Harry shopping, and stop worrying about Uncle Harry's dilemma." She then inquired, "What if he becomes incapacitated and can't function?" Then and only then should you step in without his permission and take care of him, just as you would any other sick loved one. If a child becomes ill, the parent administers the proper medicine and cares for him. When another loved one, regardless of age, is ill and needs help, render loving care *as long as there is a need*—not a minute longer.

Mr. and Mrs. A had worked hard for many years in their family business and finally retired at age sixty-two. They commuted back and forth between the South and the Midwest, and greatly enjoyed their two homes, children, grandchildren, and church work in both locations. Mrs A was constantly busy entertaining her large family and friends, and Mr. A relished hard work outdoors. Their children worried about them, but the folks were quite content. When ill health and senility hit, their children wisely kept them in their own home as long as possible and then moved each to a nursing home. These two wonderful people are now gone, but they fully enjoyed their last twenty-plus years. Their children have no regrets because they helped Mom and Dad live the way they desired during their sunset years of life.

Charley and his wife did well in business and began to circulate with the jet set. When Charley's father died, his mother, much against her will, left her Chicago apartment to reside in her son's suburban home. It soon became apparent, however, that she just *didn't fit in* with these new friends and style of life. Because her health wasn't very good, Charley moved his mother into a nursing home and, except for an occasional

visit, forgot her and his obligations. She soon
died of a broken heart, lonely and without
friends or relatives in the area. Charley could
have afforded a variety of accommodations but
didn't bother to find out what his mother really
wanted.

Alma's husband was a retired serviceman. They
owned a little house in California and really
enjoyed their comfortable at-home life. When
Alma was about seventy, her husband died, leaving her in sound financial condition. Wanting to
do the right thing and to avoid being a burden,
Alma put her son's name on all her assets in joint
ownership. Alma's daughter-in-law didn't care for
Alma and seldom visited her. In addition, Alma
was only allowed to visit them on an appointment
basis or by invitation (usually given at Thanksgiving and Christmas and lasting two hours). When
Alma began to slip physically, her son put her
into a home and took over her house and assets.
Now in her eighties, Alma is ill, bitter, and very
confused about her lot in life. She made the
mistake of turning virtually everything over to a
son who didn't love or care about her. A consul-
tation with an attorney could have produced a
trust arrangement that would have cared for her
needs in a better way. Proverbs 15:20 puts it
quite well: "A wise son maketh a glad father: but
a foolish man despiseth his mother."

Mrs. J outlived two husbands and was left
comfortably fixed by the second. She lives in her
old city neighborhood in a lovely apartment and,
although eighty, takes the bus all over town. Her
daughter, who lives in the country, wants Mrs. J

to stay with her, but Mrs. J is content to be on her own in familiar surroundings and near to her church and friends. She and her husband drew up complementary wills, since both have children by a first marriage. Life has been pleasant and active for Mrs. J, and she maintains a good relationship with all of the children.

Mrs. R's husband died a number of years ago, leaving her quite lonely and almost impoverished for about ten years. Then one day she met Mr. Y, a widower, and they fell in love. They are now happily married, have plenty of money to get along, and are both less of a problem to their children financially.

In light of these true stories, let's reconsider and paraphrase the six laws of the aged.

Law #1 indicates that allowing the elderly to retain their own life style in their chosen surroundings is important and necessary to them. Let them enjoy their remaining years in the way they desire.

Law #2 reminds us that the number one priority is their chosen home. Permit them to enjoy it as long as they can.

Law #3 won't be a problem if we simply allow older people to handle their own finances and care for their own property as long as they're capable of doing so.

Laws #4 and #5 simply state that showing we care and seeking their advice is elementary, but of great importance to oldsters.

Law #6 summarizes all of these: We must avoid trying to force our life style and opinions on elderly relations.

If we can manage to put these laws into effect in our relationships with the elderly, we will probably solve the majority of problems with our interpersonal relationships.

This is allowing the elderly to grow old gracefully and happily!

# TWO
# THE TEMPERAMENT
# OF THE AGED

It is sometimes distressing to watch the changes
that take place in bodies as they grow old. We
expect metabolic changes to occur, but in some
they seem to come more quickly, occurring even
in the fifties and sixties. Yet we run into someone
who at ninety, in rather good health, remarks
that no one else in his immediate family lived
past sixty-five. At that point our pet theories
come tumbling down. All things considered, however, we generally find that one's family "stock"
and good nutritional and health habits go a long
way toward preserving him to a ripe old age.
This seems to be generally true concerning mental health, too, but hardening of the arteries can
occur prematurely and change this as well. Psy-
chologists report that there is often a thin line
between emotional stability and mental illness, so
it behooves us to realize that we are all dependent
upon God's healing hand of blessing to maintain
our physical, emotional, *and* spiritual equilibrium
in old age.

An acquaintance of mine once boasted of his cast iron stomach, poor eating and sleeping habits, and occasional heavy drinking and smoking. At twenty-five he could brag, but at forty his health was broken from "the good life" (as he labeled it). He suffered two coronaries in a relatively short time and died at forty-two. Yet his parents and grandparents had enjoyed long lives.

By contrast, another acquaintance who performed manual labor outdoors, followed good eating habits, and came from a healthy family dropped dead while walking across the street, at thirty-seven years of age.

Several sisters in a Midwest family were one hundred to one hundred twenty-five pounds overweight, suffered from high blood pressure, and endured diabetes, as did several others in the family. They all lived fairly normal lives into their eighties, as had their parents and grandparents before them, even though some of them were diabetics too!

Mrs. J lived at home with her mother and became an alcoholic for thirty years until her mother, in her nineties, died. After her death, Mrs. J went on the wagon, became interested in life and people, and threw herself into social work. Now approaching seventy, she looks and feels well and no one can explain her good health and sharp, alert mind after thirty years of heavy drinking alone in her room night after night.

These stories illustrate some of the mysteries of the marvelous body and mind each of us has. Just as our family stock, general health traits, eating habits, and life style determine much of our physical well-being and longevity, so do temperament and emotional pattern. Dr. Tim LaHaye in his excellent book. *How to Win Over Depression*, furnishes two chapters that would be excellent reading at this point: chapter 12 on "Depression and Your Temperament" and chapter 19 on "An Eighty-Five-Year-Old Optimist."

In spite of the aging process, we *can* be optimistic because—other things remaining the same—our basic temperament doesn't change in old age. It can, however, be improved upon, and we can become more like Christ by living a Spirit-controlled life to his glory. The old flesh with its grotesque nature still haunts us, but if we by faith have received Christ as personal Savior and Lord and have been born again, his indwelling Holy Spirit can assure us of victory and blessing even in advanced age.

Proverbs 3:5, 6 and Romans 12:1, 2 are of inestimable help in this regard. Proverbs admonishes, "Trust in the Lord with all thine heart; and lean not unto thine own understanding. In all thy ways acknowledge him, and he shall direct thy paths." Romans instructs us, "I beseech you therefore, brethren, by the mercies of God, that ye present your bodies a living sacrifice, holy, acceptable unto God, which is your reasonable service. And be not conformed to this world: but be ye transformed by the renewing of your mind, that ye may prove what is that good, and acceptable, and perfect, will of God."

Notice that the pattern is identical in both passages. In Proverbs we are directed to trust in the Lord or to place implicit confidence in him with all of our being, not leaning to our own understanding or intellect for spiritual guidance. In all our ways we are to acknowledge him. This literally means: Don't go where he can't go and don't engage in anything that doesn't please him. Then he will direct your path steadily throughout life.

Please notice, too, that Romans 12 exhorts us to give over or yield our bodies to Christ for service, placing them, as it were, on the altar like a dead Old Testament sacrifice. Then we are to allow our minds to be transformed by Christ's renewing power and to refuse to be conformed to this world. Then, and only then, does God promise to allow us to see or prove out his good and acceptable and perfect will for our lives. First we yield to God and go his way; then he directs our paths. These scriptural patterns of living are especially beautiful when exhibited in old age.

Someone remarked, after looking at a silver-haired, refined Christian gentleman of eighty-five, "I wish I could be like him!" Unfortunately, Christian character doesn't come by wishing, but by being in Christ's presence and living for him year after year. Being "conformed to the image of his Son," as Paul states in Romans 8:29, is a daily, progressive sanctification or growth in godliness. What about the person suffering from hardening of the arteries who seems to become an old shrew in advanced age? Can this really happen to our sweet, kindly Christian parents? Of course it can! If the brain is damaged by strokes or an insufficient blood supply, this destroys the effectiveness of certain portions of the brain. Willpower may dwindle, resulting in unpleasant and bizarre behavior.

A man once said to me, "We'll be in old age just what we always have been spiritually, regardless of the state of our health." He also insisted, "Our minds shouldn't be affected if we've lived right." This is a ridiculous assumption for a biblically oriented believer! When we can't perform rationally because of disease and functional problems, and our old flesh is no longer controlled by a Spirit-filled temperament, it will act in its normal way, which is to allow its depraved and sinful self to surface. God will never take this old body home to glory, but will someday give us a new, resurrected, perfect body which will be incapable of sinning. The old man is "deceitful and desperately wicked: who can know it?" records Jeremiah 17:9.

Mrs. M was a generous and kind person with a real concern for others. Following a stroke, she became self-centered and jealous of her possessions, which were numerous. Instead of continuing to help others around her, she became selfish and thought only of her own security. She lived to be eighty-four and left a large estate. Yet her last few years were unhappy, self-centered ones.

By contrast, consider Mrs. R, a widow who retired in her sixties on an insurance annuity, lived in her own house until she was ninety-four years of age, and spent three more years in her daughter's home. Though her last twenty years were spent in a wheelchair, she was one of the most cheerful, young-at-heart persons I have ever met. This shows that God can perform miracles of his grace in old age, as well as before, if the mind is clear and the spirit willing.

In order to achieve spiritual victory and blessing in our later years, it is important to have fellowship with the Lord. Perhaps the greatest resource available to us after retirement is prayer. Through believing prayer, offered up in Jesus' name, one can move spiritual mountains, see needs supplied, open doors of service, see God's protective hand on loved ones, and receive strength to serve God in old age. Jeremiah 33:3 says, "Call unto me, and I will answer thee, and shew thee great and mighty things, which thou knowest not." This is just as true today as when God first promised it to Jeremiah. A corollary passage is found in the New Testament (Matt. 7:7, 8), where Jesus says, "Ask, and it shall be given you; seek, and ye shall find; knock, and it shall be opened unto you: for every one that asketh receiveth; and he that seeketh findeth; and to him that knocketh it shall be opened." This promise, too, though given over nineteen hundred years ago, is trustworthy and applicable today. If in our later years, when physical strength begins to fail, we cultivate the habit of praising God, confessing all known sin and then asking in faith for the things which we, our loved ones, our friends, church, and missionary families need, we will see God's hand moving in marvelous ways. In addition, we will have the blessing of God's fellowship and avoid the pangs of loneliness and despair so prevalent among the aged.

In the mid 1800s George Mueller of Bristol, England, supported 3000 to 5000 orphaned children by faith, praying down millions of English pounds sterling, although no foundation, missionary board, or other large organization supported him. Operating by faith, he joined with a few churches and individuals who stood with him, prayed, and gave. His work continued unabated until he reached his nineties.

With prayer and faith, Hudson Taylor founded the China Inland Mission and watched it grow into a great moving force for God. He worked closely with the group until his retirement, only four years before his death at eighty-three.

Truly God can meet our needs today if we but learn to pray in Jesus' name, in faith and with thankful hearts, expecting God to hear and answer. When all visible means of support fail, he is our refuge and strength. Faith is "the substance of things hoped for, the evidence of things not seen" (Heb. 11:1). It is far more significant than your temperament and other inherited and developed gifts, qualities, and health patterns.

Good stock and a healthy body are important gifts, but keeping in the will of God and having spiritual reserves to call upon in advanced age can be far more important. Thankfully, anyone with faith in the Lord can have these spiritual blessings to meet daily needs.

# THREE
# CHRISTIAN SERVICE
# IN RETIREMENT

At times concerned adults ask, "Should my retired parents participate in church activities?
After all, they're old now and need to take care
of themselves!" Again, these well-meaning offspring don't realize that Mom and Dad are only
older in body. Their minds are still going ninety
miles an hour and their interests, senses, and
abilities are still very much "present and account-
ed for." In most cases they don't need to slow
down but to participate actively in the things they
like best.

No dedicated believer has ever been given
enough time during his working years to accomplish all of the things that he wished in the Lord's
work. But during retirement, he is free to involve
himself as much as he likes every day. The need
is still there, the stimulus from the Lord hasn't
diminished, and his service to God can finally
proceed without interruption. No longer required
to expend his energy on an eight-hour job, to
cope with the frantic schedule of a teenager, or to

chair those interminable family council sessions, he can devote his waking hours to the Lord's work on a regular basis. Our ministry at Scott Memorial would suffer greatly if the retired people serving during the week were not available to help in every area of our program.

During retirement, the individual who enjoys fairly good health and plenty of time should make plans to accomplish all the things he has always wanted to do for the Lord. He can join the visitation and soul-winning ministries any day he wishes, baby-sit for others who desire to do visitation, help with the senior citizens' ministry, visit the church's shut-ins and the hospitalized, sing in the choir, work in the church office, send out missionary letters, do groundskeeping at Christian institutions, and help build church summer camp and missionary buildings. In other words, he can "do his thing" now that he is free, for he will only pass this way once. Remember Philippians 4:13, "I can do all things through Christ which strengtheneth me." God will grant supernatural strength to be active for him even into old age.

Young people, don't hold Mom and Dad back from actively serving the Lord, for their sake and yours. It is difficult for someone who has been busy every day for sixty-five years to suddenly have one hundred and sixty-eight hours a week to fill with no place to go or job to perform. If you desire to help your parents, in-laws, or grandparents get the most out of retirement, encourage them, long before they reach sixty-five, to become more active in their church and civic affairs, to develop hobbies, and to learn to travel for enjoyment. As a side benefit, this may protect your own life and schedule from bored family members who want to tag along on every outing, shopping excursion, and vacation.

One of the best ways to handle loneliness is to mix seniors with each other. This is why our church Live Wires (over fifty-five) group is so successful. About three years ago we started this group from scratch with a luncheon on the third Thursday of each month. Between noon and two we enjoy a fine luncheon cooked by our women, group singing, special music, slides, films, contests for fancy hats or the oldest costume, etc., and a Bible message with a gospel presentation. Seniors are encouraged to invite their friends, and we advertise in the *Senior World* newspaper. Two women in their nineties attend every luncheon, and we've grown from an average attendance of fifty to one hundred, with about two hundred different people participating. We use volunteers for table decorating and serving lunch cafeteria-style. Our folks have a wonderful time together and really enjoy the fellowship and evangelistic outreach.

In addition, we devise a monthly outing involving fifty to one hundred people. We have visited the zoo and wild animal park, set sail on a harbor cruise, visited the Navy Amphibious Base, and traveled to Palm Springs, the Queen Mary, Mt. Palomar, and many other places of interest, as well as attending the circus and Ice Capades.

We also encourage our people to get active in an adult Sunday school class, where they can have closer fellowship, make friends, and develop social and service outlets. (In fact, a widow and widower met on one of our outings, became engaged, and were recently married.) We sponsor a women's Bible class on Friday mornings, a number of missionary circles each month with day and evening meetings, and a Men's Brotherhood each month promoting fellowship and missions.

In addition, our church's college and high school offices and campuses always need volunteer workers. In the Televangelism program seniors may counsel others over the phone, lead people to Christ, and go visiting. We have discovered that useful, active, working Christians are generally happy Christians, and we feature some of the happiest believers on the face of the earth.

Recently our church began planning for a retirement center where we will be able to provide moderately priced apartments, security, transportation, and a resident nurse in order to make our folks' later years safer, more enjoyable and fruitful.

I have only touched on some of the possibilities, but let me illustrate what some of our Live Wires have accomplished.

One of our men exhibits a great deal of talent in the field of cement work. He has donated countless hours of time and labor caulking our church and school buildings and putting in cement walks, drives, and walls. Instead of easing into a rocking chair after retiring from civil service, he accepted the challenge to serve the Lord full time, and he loves it.

Another couple retired, moved to San Diego, and immediately began helping on mailings in our college and church offices. They've found real joy and blessing in helping God's work.

Mrs. J used to cook for a living. She now prepares our Live Wire luncheon each month and thoroughly enjoys it.

One of our men gets a real blessing out of helping our older ladies in and out of buses and up and down stairs (and enjoys being used of God to minister to our older folks). By no means young himself, he stays youthful by serving others.

One of our women, over eighty years of age, serves in any way possible, helping with the servicemen's center, our Televangelism ministry, and missionary circles.

Another lady, nearly ninety, is often found at the Christian Servicemen's Center, perpetuating a thirty-year ministry of kindness and love to her boys.

Old age is real, but being old is merely a state of mind which can be controlled. Many years ago two dear old servants of the Lord were discussing the process of aging. "Well, we're getting old, aren't we?" one said. The other, seventy-eight years of age, replied, "You can get old if you want to, but I'm merely getting older."

Occasionally an oldster feels sorry for himself and adopts the attitude that no one really wants him around. "I'm just in the way," he wails. These "pity parties" are very real to the senior. At such times he needs fellowship, love, encouragement and, particularly, a dynamic activity. If another senior whom he likes and respects also needs fellowship and encouragement, pair them off at an outing or a dinner. It's amazing how recreation or service to others takes our mind off our problems, real or imaginary.

If all else fails, take Mom or Dad out for a ride and a good meal. Make a little fuss over them and then ask them to do something *for* you. Pick a subject in which they have expertise and let them help you—a needlepoint or knitting problem, a business decision, a theological issue, even a plant or yard problem. We all need to feel wanted and useful, particularly to loved ones and friends. If you encourage your retired parents to be busy for Christ, they won't have time to become busybodies. This is where "Bear ye one another's burdens, and so fulfill the law of Christ" (Gal. 6:2) really becomes practical. It helps not only the senior but us as well. For, truly, if they are content and happy emotionally and spiritually, their families, in most cases, will be too.

# FOUR
# MANAGING FINANCES

Just as a large percentage of all family and marital problems seem to revolve around money, particularly in the early stages, so the problems of aging become more acute if financial pressures are severe. It used to be said that a person in retirement needed, on an average, 50 percent of his income during the peak earning years of forty through sixty. In our present inflationary economy, one probably needs closer to 60 or 70 percent of his working year's income to be comfortable, perhaps 80 or 90 percent to be well off. Very few people have this sort of income in retirement, often due to a lack of goals and proper planning. This is readily seen when we realize that 60 percent of all retirees have only Social Security to count on for their livelihood.

After retirement, conservation of estate and assets is very important because, normally, one is no longer able to build up his assets to any appreciable degree. It is therefore very necessary to try to keep intact what one has; unless, of

course, he possesses more than ample income.
This is why I mentioned in a previous chapter
that having more than adequate income in retirement should be a serious goal. If one can retire
with 25 to 30 percent more income than is needed, he can continue to accumulate cash with
interest compounded, to be used at a later date
when living costs rise or emergency expenses
come along. In this way, he may avoid having to
sell a house or other assets that he doesn't wish to
sell. Extra income can also prevent the forced sale
of stocks, bonds, or other assets at a lower price
than normally could be secured.

Through the years, I have heard many people
say, "Don't plan ahead. Just trust the Lord and
he will provide." Few of these people live well in
retirement because that general attitude spills
over into their work and saving habits, preventing
them from diligently setting goals and meeting
them. Remember the passage in Proverbs 6:6–8:
"Go to the ant, thou sluggard; consider her ways,
and be wise: Which having no guide, overseer, or
ruler, provideth her meat in the summer, and
gathereth her food in the harvest."

As surely as we're young and alive, we shall in
most cases find ourselves old and still in need of
sustenance. To be sure, God tells us not to yield
to an inordinate desire for money and things. In
1 Timothy 6:9, 10, the Bible warns, "But they
that will be rich fall into temptation and a snare,
and into many foolish and hurtful lusts, which
drown men in destruction and perdition. For the
love of money is the root of all evil: which while
some coveted after, they have erred from the

faith, and pierced themselves through with many sorrows."

The love of money and not money itself is the root of all evil; coveting after it is a sin which brings sorrows upon us. This is an entirely different matter from saving systematically out of one's earnings and planning for one's retirement. We are encouraged to bear our own burdens and supply our own needs. However illness, inflation, or other unforeseeable catastrophes may reduce us to poverty in old age, we can most certainly trust the Lord to meet our special needs.

My mother's employer used to say, "One can sleep well at night with a good fat bank account." He was a stockbroker who realized the importance of cash reserves to tide one over and to assure peace of mind.

When retiring, it is probably a good rule of thumb to convert as many assets to cash as possible (at interest, of course) or to fixed income-producing situations. In this way, funds are always available to you for "rainy days."

During the 1960s while vacationing in a Southern state, I played golf with a mobile home park owner. During our game, I asked about the average income of those who were retired and living in his park on fixed incomes. He replied that most were from Northern factory towns and had retired with factory pensions and Social Security totaling about $350.00 per month. These couples had sold their homes, bought a mobile home and a new car, and banked some cash for emergencies. In the intervening decade, inflation has threatened these couples to the extent that they would probably be in a dilemma if severe illness, car replacement, or other expensive emergencies occurred. They would be even worse off if one partner died, thus reducing their income from Social Security and pension.

In view of potential problems, it behooves each of us to plan ahead intelligently so that we can take care of our needs during our retirement years. The following suggested budgets for a couple are meant as an aid in planning for those retirement years, which will come upon most of us as surely as death and eternity, unless Christ returns first.

Please notice that income taxes, church tithes,

| MODERATE INCOME MONTHLY | | MIDDLE INCOME MONTHLY |
|---|---|---|
| $ 150.00 | Rent | $ 200.00 |
| 105.00 | Food | 130.00 |
| 25.00 | Utilities | 35.00 |
| 60.00 | Insurance | 75.00 |
| 40.00 | Doctors | 50.00 |
| 40.00 | Clothes | 50.00 |
| 35.00 | Miscellaneous | 50.00 |
| ——— | Vacation | 50.00 |
| $ 455.00 | Subtotal | $ 640.00 |
| 100.00 | With a car | 125.00 |
| $ 555.00 | | $ 765.00 |

charitable gifts, and capital expenditures are not included. Neither are extra expenses sustained in one's home, such as real estate taxes, house up-keep, lawn and garden expenses, etc. These income levels, with adjustments, would allow for comfortable living without extravagance in each category. As a rule of thumb in today's urban economy, a couple would need, with a car and an apartment or a mobile home, $6,700 for moderate income, $9,300 for middle income, and $15,000 for above average, very comfortable income in retirement.

Of course such factors as the area of the country, type of housing, cost of food and medical care, as well as state of health could change these figures dramatically. So also could living in government subsidized high rises with low monthly rent. I personally know happy and content widows who are living in small inexpensive apartments or subsidized high rise apartments on $200.00 to $300.00 per month. This, however, is the exception to the rule and would necessitate good health and low medical bills.

Generally, too, people with moderate incomes are better off if they sell their home and rent during retirement, thus gaining capital for extras and emergencies as well as increased income. Here again the preferences of the individual and his sense of well-being must be considered. Big city people often feel secure in an apartment, while small-town and country folks may need their "little house in the country" among friends, where they can grow a garden and feel secure and tranquil. Family proximity and entertaining

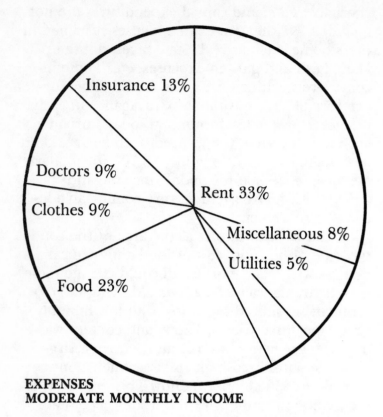

**EXPENSES**
**MODERATE MONTHLY INCOME**

make a big difference in amount of yard space and housing needs.

But how does one prepare for retirement so that adequate finances are available? A friend once told me that it wasn't what I earned but what I *saved* that mattered, and he was right. In fact, what one saves and compounds is paramount. A former missionary who lived comfortably in retirement was asked how he managed so well. He explained that he had endeavored to save 10 percent of his income throughout his

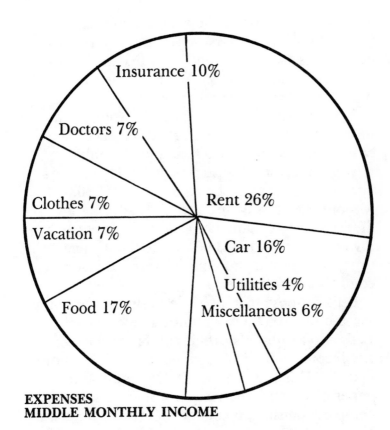

**EXPENSES**
**MIDDLE MONTHLY INCOME**

lifetime, never touching the principal or compounded interest. His father had started him on this pathway to successful retirement many years before.

At a seminar for professional people some years ago, it was demonstrated that if a young doctor would put $10,000 aside at age twenty-five, add $100 per month to this sum and invest it with a 10 percent average rate of return (principal plus interest), he would accrue $1,000,000 at sixty-five years of age. If he initiated this program at age forty-five, he would accumulate $140,000. Thus, dollars saved and invested between ages twenty-five and sixty-five are worth *seven* times the dollars saved and invested between ages forty-five and sixty-five.

A good case in point is that of a woman who inherited $10,000 at age thirty. She placed the entire amount in a savings account at only 6 percent interest per year and left it to accumulate. At age sixty-six she received over $80,000 without ever saving another nickel during her lifetime. Surely many Christians in today's economy could set aside $5,000 or $10,000 by age thirty and let it compound in order to insure a comfortable retirement.

Let's suppose that a couple desires a minimum income of $765.00 per month at age sixty-five. Let's also assume that their combined Social Security income is $475.00 per month, which is non-taxable. This leaves $290.00 per month to be generated from other sources, such as savings, company pension, income property, or an insurance annuity program. If the company pension supplies $150.00 per month, then $140.00 per month must be produced by other means. The following illustrations are not comprehensive, but they will illustrate some of the possible sources.

a) $23,000 could be put into a bank savings certificate paying 7½ percent per annum, with a resulting monthly check of $143.75, which would supply the needed income.

b) An insurance annuity or gift annuity paying approximately 8 percent could be purchased, which would also afford $140.00 per month for life with a minimum payout period of ten years but only on *one* life. An annuity can be purchased which guarantees income for both the husband and wife during their lifetimes (first one and then the other as the surviving spouse). This type of annuity, however, would pay a little less or cost a little more than $21,000.

c) United States Government E bonds could be purchased over a period of years in the amount of $28,000 and then at retirement be converted to H bonds to avoid taxes during one's lifetime. These would pay 6 percent or $1,680.00 on a semiannual basis.

d) Shares in a stock or bond mutual fund could be purchased over a period of years, and then at retirement, income could be taken on a monthly basis until the funds were entirely used up. (Generally, if 6 percent of the gross value is taken, the principal will remain intact; i.e., if $28,000 were invested and 6 percent per annum appropriated in monthly checks, $1,680.00 per year would be received without, in most cases, appreciably affecting the principal.)

e) One could purchase a duplex and live in one unit or buy a rental house which, after expenses, would yield a net of $1,680.00 per year. (A rental of $3,000 per year minus taxes, insurance, and upkeep of $1,320.00 leaves a net of $1,680.00 per year.)

f) Another route for those who do not have a company pension would be to purchase a home and have it paid for by age sixty-five. If the proceeds equal at least $48,000, this could be invested in bank certificates paying 7½ percent with a monthly or quarterly check, or 7¾ percent in a savings and loan with a monthly or quarterly check. This would provide the needed $740.00 per month with Social Security and leave $48,000 available for emergencies and final illnesses. It is also assumed that in advanced age a car and vacation could be foregone in order to help with medical expenses and the increased living costs due to inflation.

The person with a low income and without a car could, if reduced to poverty, apply for a Social Security supplement or food stamps and gain some additional help. He could also sell his home and invest the money for extra income.

In the face of all these possibilities, a systematic weekly or monthly savings program is still the key to a financially satisfactory retirement. There is no substitute for accumulating assets when one is young and healthy and when a compounding of interest will best work to one's advantage.

Sometimes when illness or other hardships have cut into one's savings, it becomes necessary to work beyond age sixty-two or sixty-five for a year or two in order to catch up and meet one's savings goal. Many times, however, it is wiser physically to work part time and to earn what one can under Social Security regulations, thus conserving one's health.

A new plan being proposed by savings institutions will provide a monthly check for home owners. At death, the amount paid plus interest compounded will be deducted from the selling price of the home. This will allow people to stay in their own homes if physically able to do so and yet use their equity for extra income. Of course, it will deplete the value of their estate and, if they live long enough, may amount to confiscation of their property at death.

It must be remembered that this chapter is not meant to be all-inclusive. A number of other routes can be tried, such as property sold on a land contract, businesses sold on ten-year notes, first and second mortgage notes, preferred stock, tax exempt municipal bonds, etc. Annuities and trusts can be set up with nonprofit organizations, which will cut taxes and also avoid some taxes because of gifts disposed during one's lifetime. Please check these out with your tax accountant, lawyer, or nonprofit institution. The development departments of Christian organizations often make their full-time personnel available to help in estate planning. It must be remembered in all financial planning for retirement that the primary aim should be safety of principal and regular income, with accessibility to funds when needed.

This conservative, sensible, no-risk approach will allow for a happier retirement and prevent sleepless nights. Oh yes, one may have to dip into the principal occasionally to cover emergency expenses, but as long as one's funds last, nothing else really matters. After all, people work hard for forty or forty-five years in order to enjoy some years of retirement together. One's money is accumulated to take care of his needs during his lifetime and not afterward. Spend it as needed and don't begrudge yourself the necessities of life. Above all, don't neglect yourself in order to leave a big estate to your heirs. Let them have

what you don't need  but take care of yourself
and the Lord's work first.

Occasionally, even Christian children squabble
over money left to charities and Christian work.
My friend Will solved the problem many years
ago by putting a provision in his will that if any
of his heirs contested the one-seventh share given
to the Lord's work, he should receive one dollar
and be cut off from all other consideration in the
will. None of his many children contested anything.

As you can see, it is important to consult a
good financial advisor and plan finances well
ahead of retirement. With our galloping inflation,
it is not enough merely to work and let retirement take care of itself. Some have said to me
that they hesitate to consult insurance men, ac-
countants, lawyers, and bankers because they all
want business or wish to sell something! This is
still far better than ending up without adequate
income at sixty-five. Somewhere along the line
you will have to seek help and trust someone.
Find a good person with an honest reputation
and listen to him, but never put all of your eggs
in one basket. Spread your investments out—
insurance, real estate, bank deposits, pension system, trust deeds, stocks, bonds, and government
bonds. With adequate diversification you can
avoid getting hurt too badly at any one time.
Then sit back, enjoy life, and let your assets grow
and compound while you work, play, and enjoy
serving the Lord.

Manage your finances. Never let them manage
you.

# FIVE
# COPING WITH INFLATION

An average retired couple in a Southern mobile
home park was able to live on $350.00 per month
ten years ago. Now they are pinched at $600.00
per month, and expectations for the future are
not encouraging. Dollars saved today are losing 5
to 10 percent of their value per annum, which
means that the cost of living is rising by that
amount each year. Because of this, the goal set
for one's retirement may be only one-half or
one-quarter of the amount needed in forty years.
Therefore, savings must be adjusted periodically.

Of course, many pension systems, as well as
Social Security, have built-in automatic increases
as the cost of living rises, but these are often not
enough to cover needs. It is wise to put aside a
little more than is needed and to plan, if possible,
for 25 percent or more income above what one
feels he or she may require. (Or you might build
up a good cash "kitty" to be set aside for increased or extraordinary expenses.) This is another reason why a house has always been an

excellent investment, for it increases in value and provides a hedge against inflation.

Real estate taxes, on the other hand, also increase and may eventually push older people with fixed incomes out of their homes. The cash from the home's sale is then available for income, purchase of a mobile home, and extra expenses. Homes in good residential neighborhoods hold their values best. Homes in shabby and run-down areas may actually decrease in value. Location is thus an all-important factor.

Mr. L bought a home in a nice area, but the area changed and became run down. By the time he sold the house, the value had decreased from $15,000 to $12,000. His retirement balloon had been deflated.

Mrs. R owned an older home in a good, stable neighborhood. In thirty years, its value soared from $12,000 to $65,000. This increased value now provides Mrs. R with tremendous reserves if she ever needs to sell her home.

Another so-called inflation hedge that hasn't worked too well is industrial stocks. Many are now selling at one-half to two-thirds of their value ten years ago. If one needed money now and had to sell, it could be tragic. Mrs. B was left stock by her husband, but when expensive surgical bills developed, she had to sell some of it. Mrs. B found that her forty-dollar shares were now worth only twenty-five dollars. In addition, her income suffered when she sold the shares to pay her bills.

Many low-interest bonds have also depreciated in value because of low interest rates. If sold now, they would bring only 70 to 80 percent of the original value. They will eventually be redeemed at face value, but if sold before then would give the investor a loss.

This reminds me of the story of a large, famous church which sold bonds to build its new facility in the late 1920s. Many members said that they didn't trust churches and chose rather to put their money in the banks. When scores of banks failed in the 1930s, some of these same people lost a great deal of money, but not one person who bought the church's bonds forfeited interest or principal. It was a good investment from two points of view: safety of principal and safety of return. Both are important in any investment program.

Dr. Tim LaHaye tells of a banker who loaned money to hundreds of churches over a thirty-year period. The banker testified, "I do not know of one church that failed to pay its debts." He mentions that even during the Depression, when banks closed and people often lost everything, the churches paid off every dollar even though reimbursement was sometimes delayed.

Some insurance policies and annuities pay only 2½ percent per year minus administration fees. These are a poor savings and accumulation vehicle. Many group tax-sheltered annuities are paying 6 to 8 percent interest and more on principal paid in, and they offer larger returns at age sixty-five than individual policies. Be sure to talk to an independent insurance broker about policies advanced by different companies. Change companies or roll over your account when more favorable rates are available elsewhere on tax-sheltered annuities.

Inflation has also hit hard at health care costs. Hospital room expenses, for example, have increased five to ten times in the past ten to fifteen years, and doctors' fees are skyrocketing at almost the same rate. In retirement, therefore, supplementary health care insurance above Medicare should be carried, if possible, in order to cover 65 to 80 percent of all medical costs.

Inflation has also caused increases in utilities, gasoline and car expenses, food prices, and even vacation expenses. One must either make proper allowances or continue working part time in order to supplement retirement income.

Governmental agencies seem to be primarily concerned with minority groups, the impoverished, the blind, deaf, lame, and unskilled. These groups are certainly needy, but what about those who have cared for their own needs through the years, and then have run out of money in old age? As taxpaying citizens, they are deserving of consideration and help—before they become impoverished. When they have finally used up all of their assets, it will cost more to maintain them because their income-producing principal is gone.

Scott Memorial Baptist Church is trying to relate to these needs (without government aid) and to be supportive and helpful. Very often, however, the pioneer spirit prevails, and our seniors refuse to let anyone know of their present or impending needs. Recently, one woman said that she wouldn't think of using the Lord's money for her own necessities. When it was pointed out to her that the deacon's fellowship offering was taken each month during the communion service for that purpose, she replied, "I know it, but I still don't want any of it. The Lord will provide for me just as he has in the past!"

For those who didn't start saving early enough in life and who are now in trouble because of inflation, the following steps can be taken.

Liquidate any low- or non-income producing property or assets in order to get cash which can then be invested in certificates of deposit or an insurance annuity policy. This will give extra income in the years ahead. It may involve selling one's house, stamp or coin collection, family heirlooms, or jewelry. It may also mean cashing in some notes or bonds at a discount or selling some vacant land in order to have cash to invest.

A Social Security supplement can be obtained for low-income couples; or, if in good health, a retiree can often work part-time in order to enjoy a more comfortable living. One can earn up to $4,000 per year without losing Social Security benefits, and this figure is being increased by the recently passed Social Security bill.

In addition, children can help their parents with a monthly check, remembering that their parents spent $20,000–$40,000 raising and educating them. In many cultures of the world, care of the elderly is expected. For some reason, we in America tend to ignore our elders' needs instead of trying to meet them.

So much for the impact of inflation upon our economy, income, and assets. What will happen in the years to come is almost anybody's guess.

Even a so-called moderate 4 percent of inflation per year means that most young people planning for retirement in thirty or forty years will need to project two or three times more income than is needed at present. The best approach is to install a realistic savings program, plan ahead for retirement, and then put the rest in the hands of the Lord. Those who know Christ as personal Savior and Lord and who are living in obedience to him can say with the Apostle Paul in Philippians 4:13, 19, "I can do all things through Christ which strengtheneth me"; and "My God shall supply all your need according to his riches in glory by Christ Jesus." This is truly the believer's source of security. Learn to carry your burdens to the Lord and then leave them there.

# SIX
# ADULT CHILDREN'S
# FINANCIAL NEEDS

In any discussion of the problems of aging, it is essential that we also discuss the finances and health of the retiree's children. This can become a serious issue and can have tragic consequences if it is not properly handled.

At times, a child may develop a debilitating disease or financial problems which render him less able to care for himself than are his aged parents. Just how should parents view this situation and how should they respond? One's financial abilities help to determine a course of action. A parent is not expected to go bankrupt to care for one adult son or daughter to the neglect of the other children. Even the prodigal son, though given a banquet on his return, didn't get back his dissipated inheritance. The remainder of Dad's goods went to the other brother.

In certain cases, a child may be handicapped, or else develop a physical problem in later life and become handicapped. This is a completely different situation, and in such a case everyone in the family should help, realizing that "there, but for the grace of God, go I." The supportive family is in complete obedience to Galatians 6:2, "Bear ye one another's burdens, and so fulfill the law of Christ."

Mary contracted polio at age fifteen and was completely paralyzed except for one hand, her head and neck. The whole family pitched in to assist financially and physically. Besides helping financially, one brother even came 2,000 miles several times a year to spend time with her. Because of her supportive family, Mary's life was a cheerful one, even in the midst of such adverse circumstances. Though she died several years later, she lived a fulfilled life because others cared for her and responded to her needs.

George worked very hard for thirty years to build up his business. He then sold it and retired in his sixties. Soon after George's retirement, his son contracted multiple sclerosis and slowly began to lose control of his muscles. George and his wife, his family, and her family were all in good financial positions. The father wanted his son and daughter-in-law to live near him so he could help with his son during the day, but they preferred to stay in their rural home and enjoy the animals and peaceful surroundings. George wisely left them alone and has been as supportive as possible from a distance. Because of this, all three families lead very normal lives and get along superbly, without disruptive problems. Later on, circumstances may change, but at present everyone has wisely chosen to move slowly.

Mr. A was a hard working, thrifty European

who loaned one of his daughters money that was never repaid. Upon his death some twenty-five years later, he deducted this amount from her inheritance and gave an extra share to a son who lived nearby and cared for his business. The family (except for the daughter) was satisfied and thought that Mr. A had treated them all fairly.

Mr. T retired with substantial assets and then became a widower. He doted on one of his children, and kept giving him financial aid until he had completely used up his means. Mr. T was forced to ask his other child for help. This child was highly incensed because Dad had given away his inheritance as well and was now asking him for support. Mr. T was not fair and impartial to his children.

Retired parents should not cosign notes for their adult offspring. If able, give them the money or loan it to them with an interest-bearing note. If you cosign their commercial loans, you may end up paying the bill when you're not able to do so. This also applies to grandchildren. If there's anything worse than going broke at sixty-five, it's having to be supported by one's children. Being self-sufficient and independent is a great blessing and should not be jeopardized. Of course, we are not speaking of the wealthy retiree, but of the average parent of limited means who wants to retire with dignity and remain independent.

Sometimes the unexpected happens, and children who were very well off financially suffer business reverses or even go bankrupt in middle age. Mr. and Mrs. L had a son who was a millionaire, and they considered leaving him out of their wills. Their attorney advised against it, saying that one never knows what the future will bring. They wisely listened and set up a trust for their children to share equally. Shortly after the parents passed away, the well-to-do son went bankrupt due to business reverses. His only remaining income came from the family estate. By being fair and treating all of their children the same, Mr. & Mrs. L were able to provide for a need they could not possibly have anticipated.

Our parents are a source of financial advice that we often overlook. We tend to forget that Dad and Mom have gained a great deal of knowledge through experience and that we can avoid many bumps in life by profiting from what they have learned. It may be that Dad faced exactly the same dilemma we are facing (although he may not have mentioned it) and solved it successfully. Why not borrow from his experience—or Mom's or Grandpa's—and save ourselves a headache or two?

Mr. Z began working in a bank as a teller in his early twenties and eventually became president. He had eight children and wanted to treat all of them alike, which was difficult because some lived near him, and their needs and demands were heard most often. As he approached eighty, fighting began over his large estate and private collection of antiques. In order to avoid undue squabbling, Mr. Z arranged his will in the following way: He gave a portion to charity, established a lifetime income and cash stipend for each of his children, and called in a professional auctioneer to appraise all of his household possessions, antiques, and books.

Then each of his children was allowed to come in and pick out what he or she wanted from his possessions, and the price marked on it was deducted from the cash stipend mentioned in the will. Beginning with the eldest and working down to the youngest, each took what he or she could afford; the remainder was sold and the proceeds applied to the estate. The children seemed to be pleased, and everything went well because Mr. Z did all that he could to avoid dissension after his death. As an auctioneer of estates once put it, "You can really tell who the good Christians are when the time comes to settle the estate in the lawyer's office." With a little prudence and sanctified good sense, estate squabbles and unhappy heirs can be avoided.

Mrs. A had several daughters-in-law and a number of granddaughters who each wanted some of her beautiful cut glass and painted plates and bowls. In order to let each one have what she really wanted, Mrs. A began, several years before her death, to give favorite pieces to her daughters-in-law and granddaughters. Now, many years after her death, I have yet to hear of one argument about her antiques. A very wise mother-in-law and grandmother used her head and had fun conferring all of her beautiful things upon those who would most appreciate them.

As has been shown, it is important to keep one's financial affairs in order after retirement.

By doing this, the parent is able to provide assistance when needed and to avoid hard feelings, while keeping his own income intact. May God help us as families to work together to solve our problems in God's appointed way, which is with loving hearts of compassion.

# SEVEN
# HOUSING AND
# RELATED EXPENSES

Next to the cost of health care, food, and automobiles, housing is fast becoming a major trouble spot in the retiree's budget. Newer, modern apartments used to be available in Arizona, Florida, and California for $75 to $125.00 per month. An adequate one-bedroom apartment today is priced at $150.00 to $225.00, and two-bedroom modern apartments are $190.00 to $275.00 and up. This is particularly a dilemma for single women over sixty-five years of age with only $200.00 to $300.00 total monthly income, usually from Social Security and interest on a few dollars in savings.

In some cities, certain government-subsidized high-rise apartment buildings rent for a maximum of 25 percent of one's income, which is a great help. In other areas, however, these are not available. When they are, they provide fellowship, security, a social program, elevators, and proximity to transportation and stores.

During retirement, it is absolutely essential that housing costs be less than one-third of one's income. Also, avoid making mortgage payments on a house unless absolutely essential (and only in proper balance with income). The rules, of course, change when we have ample resources and income, since taxable income will determine the best course of action. The rapid increase in house prices and a probable desire to sell and take capital gains in a few years might also necessitate a mortgage on the property in order to insure a tax benefit for the seller while owning it; and for the buyer, who probably would want to assume the mortgage and add to it. Some are fortunate enough to have low-interest Veterans Administration or Federal Housing Administration assumable loans, and may not want to pay them off if they are getting a bigger return on their money in a lending institution or other investment.

As one can readily see, it is necessary to study the financial picture at retirement in the light of income, assets, tax bracket, long-term estate objectives, required housing, spending habits, and other related needs, as well as family involvement. Those of ample means and assets should sit down with their accountant and attorney and do some serious estate planning *prior* to retirement. Some who retire at fifty-five or sixty still have children in high school or college whom they want to continue helping. Adequate planning for this should be undertaken long before retirement arrives.

I have found that some people dearly love

yardwork, gardening, and housework. They thrive on being busy and take great pride in maintaining a beautiful lawn and "show place" yard and house. To them extensive travel, entertainment, car, clothes, and other "luxury expenses" are not nearly as important as a nice-looking, comfortable home and yard. If you are one of these, plan ahead so that you can keep your present home or purchase a smaller but still comfortable place, and be happy in retirement.

One of the greater blessings and rewards of owning property today can come from a garden. A large vegetable garden can really cut down on the year-round food bill if products are canned and frozen.  In rural areas, where one can keep some livestock and where fishing and hunting are good, retirees can often raise, catch, and shoot most of their food and thus tremendously cut their expenses. In addition, if wood is readily available for a fireplace, the heating bill can be minimized except in very cold weather. Doors and windows can be insulated and caulked extensively to save on heating bills. Heavily lined drapes will also sharply reduce heat loss through windows.

Since we live in sunny San Diego where the weather is mild, we have found that with extensive insulation, heavily lined drapes, and solar heat via the east windows in the morning, we can get by during most of the winter with only fireplace heat. During the mild winter of 1976–77, we did not turn on our heat after December 1, though we did use the fireplace eight or ten times. By also conserving water, electricity, and gas, one can cut his bills by 20 to 30 percent in one year.

Though we tend to respect the homeowner who babies his garden and manicures his lawn, some people can't be bothered with a house and yard. They are much happier traveling, working in church programs, and assisting civic organizations. Apartment living is just right for them. Besides, water and heat are often furnished as part of the rent, making the utility bill small indeed.

The old adage, "know thyself," is appropriate here. If more husbands and wives would discuss their feelings, expectations, and goals before retirement and let their children know of their decisions, a large number of unhappy situations would be avoided.

In addition to the type of housing desired, there is the problem of where to locate geographically. Let me illustrate. One couple from New Jersey had always wanted to live in a warmer climate during retirement so they would not be cooped up during the winter. They sold their home and bought a duplex in south Florida. However, within six months they were miserable, bickering wrecks. Why? Because the wife had lived for her children and grandchildren and actually had developed no life or interests of her own. She was not involved in hobbies, despised yard work, didn't mix well with others, and hated everything about her beautiful duplex. Within a year and a half her doctor advised them to return to New Jersey to be near the "kids."

That's exactly what they did, and now she's as

happy as a lark. What about her husband? Well, he has so many interests and hobbies that location really doesn't make much difference to him. In fact, he works part-time at his old job, using his machining skills, and can therefore afford to visit Florida in the winter. Consequently, they now have the best of two worlds because they are back in their church, ethnic neighborhood, and club, yet can afford to spend some weeks each year in a temperate climate.

On the opposite side of the coin is a couple from Chicago who had always loved California and hated the cold Northern winters. As soon as Jim became sixty-two, they headed West, gravitated to a smaller town, and became active in a church. They never missed Chicago a bit. Occasionally they go back to visit their daughter, but they are well adapted to their new mobile home. Thus, the location and type of housing are not nearly so important as knowing oneself and one's mate, planning ahead, and establishing goals which are attainable and which will meet one's needs.

Some years ago, an elderly woman sold her home and moved in with her son and daughter-in-law. Almost from the beginning tensions and problems mounted. Mrs. S was unhappy because no one wanted her and she was forced to live in a strange suburban area with few elderly around her. She would have been far happier in her denominational retirement home, where she really had wished to live, but her son was more concerned about the financial outlay than Mother's happiness. So they were all miserable together. When her son retired and moved away, he put her in a nursing home and left her up North *alone* until she died.

Another woman lived for forty years in a rural farm area. In her sixties she went to stay with her two daughters, residing six months in each of their homes. In both cases they enjoyed Mom and tried to make her happy, but she still missed the country and wanted to live on the farm. They would probably *all* have been much happier had her daughters sent her home to the farm in the summer and brought her back to their homes in the winter so that she could visit old friends for a few months out of the year. In this case, she had virtually no money, but her prosperous sons-in-law were able to help her. Fortunately they are all Christians and have tried to resolve the problems, but difficulties still exist.

I realize that this is a tremendously complex problem. With rapidly rising property values and taxes, it is not easy to stabilize one's housing expenses. When it becomes necessary, moving into smaller quarters may cut the overhead just enough for one to get by. Purchasing a smaller home or moving from a two-bedroom to a one-bedroom apartment or efficiency could make the difference between just existing and enjoying life. Self-discipline and lack of rigidity in values can help us make the necessary adjustments when needed.

Sometimes children and parents working together can solve the housing problem with benefits for all parties concerned by buying a duplex or two houses on one lot together, sharing housing and expenses in this way. This also allows Dad to putter and keep things "fixed." Two sisters who are alone could rent a small house or two-bedroom apartment and cut expenses by not paying two rents. They could also get by with one car rather than two.

When seeking solutions, take counsel together as a family and then prayerfully ask God to reveal the best answer. He has promised "to supply all of our needs," and that guidance will be forthcoming if we seek it from the Lord.

It is also possible to find towns (outside of metropolitan areas) where rents are modest and one can walk to shopping, church, library, etc., rather than use the car for everything. In rural areas, vegetables can often be purchased at a lower price. All of these adjustments can cut expenses and help make ends meet.

# EIGHT
# HEALTH PROBLEMS

As folks grow older, their bodies begin to change. Some bodies change rapidly, others more slowly. Hardening of the arteries, elevated blood pressure, or heart disease plague some people. Others confront cataracts, loss of ability to hear, arthritis, diabetes, etc. Of one fact all of us can be sure— we will face infirmity in the flesh if we live long enough.

How should you react when your aging body begins to show signs of wear? Adapt to the difficulty, but keep on going. Instead of collapsing on a bed of self-pity and lamenting your fate, prolong your love affair with life and continue to serve the Lord.

One woman loved gardening, but an enlarged heart and accompanying fatigue made her unable to spend long periods of time out in the sun in her yard. Her son decided to curtail her activities and keep her indoors most of the time. A wise physician, however, permitted her to go out earlier in the morning. About 10 A.M., when the heat began in earnest and she began to feel tired, she was to go inside and lie down for a rest. The doctor told her to stay out of the sun and to work indoors or in the shade the remainder of the day. Because the doctor was wise enough to adapt his patient's health requirements to her environment and need, she is, twelve years later, a happy, outgoing, active octogenarian instead of a frustrated, ulcer-ridden old shrew. The doctor also instructed the son to leave his mother alone and let her lead an active, fulfilled life. What made the difference for this lady? A wise and concerned doctor who treated the whole person with common sense and helped her adapt to her limitations.

A Christian friend had to retire at sixty-two because of heart trouble. Being active and energetic, he dreaded the thought but had no choice. Moving to a warmer climate, he began to help his newfound church build its Christian education building. When he became tired, he went home and rested. The activity strengthened his heart and body, and he was soon in better health than when he retired. This is adaptation in its finest sense.

One of our ladies lost her eyesight in her forties but refused to give up. After learning Braille and developing other skills, she was greatly used in our offices for many years. Until recently, she did stapling, calling, piano playing, and special projects for the church. Though retired, nearing seventy, and not in the best of health, she is still a vibrant, happy Christian. This is adaptation.

One day a middle-aged couple asked me what to do with their aged, senile parent. They were torn by love and duty, and yet could not adequately care for the sickly woman who needed so much attention. They wanted to keep her at home with them, but it wasn't working out and all of them were miserable. When I visited the home, I could clearly see that no one could cope with this irrational, bizarre-acting invalid at home. Mother wandered at night, with or without clothes, turned on the gas, eliminated at will, and generally made a nuisance of herself. It was long past time to commit her to a properly staffed nursing facility where she would get better care than at home. Overseeing one's parents and honoring them doesn't mean that one must do it at home, regardless of the toll in family relationships, health, and living standards. Often the best care can be found in a well-equipped nursing facility. Being a martyr may invigorate our emotions temporarily, but it is detrimental to Mom and Dad, spouse, and family in the long run.

Because you must answer to the Lord for your actions, ask him for guidance. Request Christian friends to pray with you, talk to your pastors and family doctor, and then do what's best for your aged relative—don't just follow your feelings.

Proverbs 3:5, 6 can be a blessing at such a time. The writer says, "Trust in the Lord with all thine heart; and lean not unto thine own understanding. In all thy ways acknowledge him, and he shall direct thy paths."

The main thing to remember when putting loved ones in a home or hospital is to visit regularly, bring in the youngsters occasionally, and, wherever possible, bring them home for dinner and out for a ride or stroll. This will benefit all concerned and will meet many of their needs. A ninety-five-year-old woman whom I once served used to thrive on her weekly ride with her son. She lived for little else all week. He had given up trying to take care of her needs at home but was faithful in visiting her at the nursing home. This made her weekend and kept her happy and content.

In general, associating with people of one's own age group, as well as seeking close daily companionship, will keep one far happier than remaining home, alone and in the family's way.

Someone over seventy with all his faculties is just as sensitive to the needs around him as you are. He is also conscious of his diminishing physical strength. Help your aged loved ones to cope with and find new outlets, letting them know that you understand their needs and frustrations. Because they love you and want your approval, this is often a bigger contribution to their well-being than giving them money, furnishing possessions, or providing an increased standard of living as part of your home and life style.

Another suggestion which pays big dividends is: insist that your aged parents have physical examinations periodically, or at least be regularly attended by a physician who specializes in internal medicine. This will keep them in as good health as possible, and well-functioning bodies will usually make old age a blessing instead of a painful ordeal. The doctor will most likely prescribe proper vitamins and minerals; and important blood tests for blood sugar, cholesterol, calcium and phosphorous levels, etc., will be periodically ordered, in addition to electrocardiograms and urinalyses. These periodic physicals, along with adequate eye examinations by a competent optometrist or ophthalmologist, regular dental checkups, good personal hygiene, and an adequate diet are most important for a happy, healthy retirement.

Good doctors are best found by recommendations through other respected doctors in the area. One can also call the local dental, medical, or optometric association for contacts, but personal referrals are best.

One of the greatest difficulties for the elderly is a lack of proper diet and poor eating habits. This is particularly true when the elderly person is alone. It is difficult to cook a full meal for one person because the leftovers last all week and make the diet monotonous. In addition, a single person doesn't need three big meals a day, and therefore an adequately balanced diet often is not present.

Some elderly singles go out for a good meal at noon in order to get at least one balanced meal with fresh vegetables each day. With a regular regimen of personal care—vitamins and minerals to supplement one's diet, cereals and bread with good fiber content, fresh fruit, adequate fluids, and exercise—the average senior can enjoy many healthy years even into the eighties and nineties. Our Live Wires (over fifty-five) prove this to be true because so many of them are healthy, active, and living in their own apartments at seventy-five, eighty, and even ninety-five years of age.

Yes, your body may change and endure a few aches and pains, but good preventive medicine, adequate diet, exercise, and common sense will, with God's help, make retirement years the best years.

# NINE
# HOBBIES IN RETIREMENT

I am constantly amazed at the lack of hobbies and interests on the part of so many older people! Too many of them are only interested in their work, house, yard, and family, often in that order. When these busy, hard-working people reach sixty-five, retire from their jobs, sell their homes, and move into a mobile home or apartment in Florida, Arizona, or California, their troubles suddenly begin. Dad is always under Mom's feet (he was always there before, but Mom just never noticed him). Mom is never ready to go anywhere (she was probably late many times before, but Dad never paid much attention). And finally, the "kids," meaning the grandchildren, are hundreds of miles away. Now, how in the world do you solve this dilemma? Why, with new interests and hobbies, of course.

Long before retirement ever looms on the horizon, and preferably in younger years, one ought to begin developing interests other than work, yard, house, and family. These things are important, because as the years go by and times change, so will interests, job, and childrens' needs. Wise is the couple who begins to cultivate other interests and hobbies. Gardening together is a healthy pastime, but indoor winter hobbies are needed as well. Whether it be knitting or crocheting blankets, weaving rugs, collecting coins or stamps, becoming a rock hound or lapidary, expanding sports interests, fishing and hunting together, taking up painting or button collecting, it is important to develop other interests. In fact, the more the merrier—within reason.

Many folks think it is difficult to expand their interests. On page 76 is a list of some hobbies and outside interests, and places where such activities may be learned and enjoyed. Remember, we are never too old to learn. Grandma Moses, Dwight Eisenhower, and Winston Churchchill all began painting late in life and were successful at it. Many of these hobbies can be started now at little or no cost and can be enjoyed during retirement as time and finances permit.

A husband and wife should share one or two hobbies such as gardening, painting, or golf in the summer; and stamps, coins, antiquing, or bowling in the winter. Travel, fishing, and rock hunting pursuits during the summer can be combined with winter evenings reserved for slide shows, making "flies," and rock polishing or stone setting.

Even the restoration of an old house could be a recreative project, taking a year or two at the onset of retirement. Whatever your hobbies, however, remember that you will probably reside in smaller quarters when retired, and thus storage space will be at a premium. Coin and stamp collecting are popular with older people because very little space is needed to store one's collection. Gardening, too, can be done in one's own yard and is, therefore, satisfying as well as utilitarian.

One retired couple had always wanted to travel but had not previously taken the opportunity. When they retired, they spent about four weeks in a different state each year and really enjoyed seeing all they could. They soon were sought after for travel talks and became interested in history as a sideline. They learned to love and appreciate America all the more and were much better conversationalists wherever they went. In fact, when they met other retired people, they invariably could say, "We've been in your state" or county or town. This helped open doors and make many new friends.

Remember, your time is precious because you will never pass this way again. Make the most of it and be a good steward of the time and talents entrusted to you.

Our Live Wires at Scott Memorial are so busy and active for the Lord that they seldom have time to get bored. By keeping energetic and alert, they avoid self-pity and keep right on producing fruit in old age. Many of them have developed hobbies which take care of spare hours and give much pleasure. One of our ladies crochets fancy potholders and gives them away as gifts. They are much appreciated and sought after because they are handmade.

A retired doctor friend in another state lives on

| | | |
|---|---|---|
| Dressmaking and suitmaking | Work, play, dress | Night school, community centers, senior citizens' clubs, sewing centers |
| Figurines | By countries, armed forces, animals, birds, fish, fruit, men, women, historical | Department and porcelain stores, antique shops, old world shops, Austria, Bavaria, Germany |
| Fishing | Deep sea, fresh water inland waterways, casting, trolling | Local lakes, oceans, rivers, streams, private fish farms and preserves |
| Gardening | Flowers, fruit, shrubs, vines, foliage, ground cover, indoor, African violets, hydroponic, ultraviolet, oriental, vegetable | Garden clubs, florists, nurseries, own yard, oriental florists, catalogue seed companies |
| History buff | By country, topic, world, family, political, business | County historical societies, historical sites, libraries, museums, old book shops |
| Hunting | Small game, big game, gun, bow and arrow, trapping, fowl | All over the world |
| Lapidary | Gem stones, paper weights, bookends, unique, historical | High school and community college classes, community centers, rock clubs, rock shops, throughout the world |

| HOBBY | TYPES | SOURCES |
|---|---|---|
| Art | Oil, watercolor, ink, etc. | Adult classes at high schools, colleges, community centers, senior citizens' clubs, and private art galleries |
| Antiques | Glass, furniture, clocks, paintings, rugs, bowls, etc. | Antique shops, house and garage sales, dealers' stores, and flea markets |
| Books | Topical, rare, historical | Secondhand books, house and rummage sales, libraries, bookstores |
| Buttons | Antique, topical, bone, glass, metal, patriotic, etc. | Thrift shops, Salvation Army stores, antique shops, department and fabric stores |
| Cameos | Shell, bone, ivory | Antique shops, jewelers, Italy |
| Coins | Old, new, types, topical by country, worldwide | Coin clubs, auctions, dealers, antique shops, garage sales |
| Dolls | Old, new, country, costumed | Department stores, antique shops, garage sales, Goodwill stores |

| HOBBY | TYPES | SOURCES |
|---|---|---|
| Matchbook covers | Topical, hotels, motels, resorts, trains, ships, restaurants | Restaurants and other public places |
| Old clocks and watches | By country, maker, wood or brass, movement | Antique shops, house sales, farm auctions, other collectors, pawn shops, jewelry stores featuring antique jewelry |
| Old maps | Country, county, state, historical, military | Antique shops, book dealers |
| Photography | Still, movie, 35 mm, black & white | Community centers, photography clubs, adult education classes, photographic shops |
| Postcards | Special day (Christmas, Easter, etc.), historical, topical, country, scenic | On trips, drugstores, card shops, restaurants, motels, hotels, depots, collectors, stamp shops, post offices |
| Records | Classical, religious, etc. | Record shops, antique shops, music stores, garage sales, etc. |

| | | |
|---|---|---|
| Rock hunting | Gem stones, paper weights, bookends, unique, historical | All over the country, in rock shops, from collectors and lapidaries |
| Rug weaving | Varied | Adult evening school, community colleges, community centers, wool shops |
| Sculpturing | People, animals, events, topics, birds, ships | Community centers, adult night schools, community colleges, art galleries, private teachers |
| Stamps | Country, topical, event, people, commemorative, airmail, revenue, proprietary, etc. | Stamp clubs, shows, auctions, dealers, post offices, collectors, garage sales, antique shops |
| Sports | Bowling, golf, tennis, sailing, swimming, badminton, shuffleboard, Ping-Pong, pool, handball | |
| Travel | To various places each year or interesting short trips each week or month | Privately or through travel clubs or agencies or senior citizens' clubs |

a lake and goes fishing every morning at day-
break when it is cool. After catching fish for
lunch, he works in the yard among his hybrid day
lilies until the sun gets too hot. He then goes
indoors for breakfast, letter writing, and mail
time. Over eighty years of age, he is president of
his garden club and his homeowners' association.
His yard, flowers, and bird watching mean a
great deal to him and keep him completely happy
and satisfied, even though he is alone much of
the time.

You, too, can be happy and satisfied in retirement if you will plan ahead and prepare hobbies
and interests for the day when you will have
more time than money.

# TEN
# HOW TO AFFORD A VACATION ON RETIREMENT INCOME

Have you noticed how some seniors enjoy their later years? They seem to have fun together, engage in a variety of activities, and even take an occasional trip or vacation. Everyone on the block wonders how they do it! "Is it possible that they're loaded?" a friend wonders. No, he discovers, their income is modest and their assets quite limited. Yet they take regular trips and vacations, whereas their contemporaries can't seem to stretch the dollars far enough to do so. How do they manage? In most cases, a little planning (and perhaps a bit of self-denial) serves far better than a fat bank account. Vacations in retirement are distinctly possible for those who really want them. Oh, they may not take place in a new $30,000 motor home or a Cadillac, but they will be delightful!

Some folks plan for a vacation within their regular budget. They put aside five or ten dollars a week in a separate account earmarked for special outings. This money draws interest and builds up during the year, thus accumulating an impressive fund. Others put a lump sum into a savings account when they retire, then use only the *interest* for vacations. This affords them a perpetual fund to pay for their excursions. Still others make some handmade articles and sell them to friends for Christmas presents. In this way, they build up their vacation kitty.

One friend takes care of two lawns in the neighborhood and uses this money for vacations. Another woman faithfully saves her occasional baby-sitting money. Others use birthday and anniversary gifts from relatives for this purpose.

One couple sells some of their coins and stamps each year. Their collection of thirty years provides sufficient funds for vacations and outings without cutting into their budget.

Another retired couple cleans the showroom and offices of an automobile dealer each morning from five to eight A.M. These folks utilize their income for car and travel expenses.

A retired gardener raises vegetables for several people in his neighborhood and gets paid for it. He, too, uses these funds for his vacation.

A former maintenance man in a factory is now a church custodian. He earns over two hundred dollars a month, which he uses for extra drug bills, clothing expenses, and trips. These excursions often take this man and his wife to a lake where they can fish.

As you can see, there is no end to the variety of means by which one can supplement his retirement income. This makes it possible to take some excellent vacations. It does, however, demand some planning!

After you accumulate the money, then what? Where can you go for an enjoyable vacation without having it cost an arm and a leg? Much depends on your tastes and needs. If you're in good health and like to rough it, there are plenty of superior fishing and camping spots that are reasonable. Of course, you may have to set up a tent, rent a small older cottage, or bring your camper or travel trailer. Living space and food for two will run from five to fifteen dollars per day with these accommodations, if you do your own cooking.

If your tastes are more refined, the experience will be more costly. A nice tourist home, motel, or hotel will increase your costs thirty to fifty dollars per day for lodging and meals in a restaurant.

Travel expenses will average fifteen to twenty-five cents per mile by car or camper plus entertainment and sightseeing expenses. By knowing the mileage involved, one can approximate the cost of a vacation. Why not plan ahead and save for a specific trip? Of course, if you have friends or relatives in a desirable area, you can easily trade off visits. In that way, you can cut down tremendously on vacation expenses. It all depends upon what you want and are willing to save toward. Discipline yourself in order to obtain and enjoy these little luxuries.

Some very good maps and information may be obtained through automobile clubs, travel agencies, chambers of commerce, national and state parks, state visitors' bureaus, airlines, etc. One of the best ways to hold costs down is to concentrate on one city or area and to take tours or trips within a fifty-mile radius from reasonably priced lodging. Sometimes two couples go together, rent a cottage on a lake, and share expenses. This always helps the budget and provides a special dimension of close fellowship with friends.

Some senior citizens' groups offer reasonably priced one- to three-week tours to various parts of the United States as well as to Canada, Mexico, Alaska, Hawaii, Europe, and Central America. The advantages of traveling in a group with a tour guide leader are many. Tickets and luggage are handled, safe travel is to be expected, the most interesting areas are explored, and good accommodations and meals are included. In addition, you will pay only a stated price, with no additional shocks to the pocketbook unless self-induced. Many times a ten-day trip to Europe for two can be less expensive than a ten-day vacation in the States. Why? Because of group wholesale rates to travel agencies, as well as a more favorable dollar conversion rate in such countries as England and Spain.

Even if you can't see your way clear for a long trip, why not plan ahead for a four- or five-day outing within 500 miles of home? With careful planning, you can work out the details and enjoy a delightful vacation on your limited resources.

Even short weekend trips are nice, particularly when one visits relatives or friends. These visits to their areas are not costly, and there is a good opportunity for fellowship.

If even short trips are an economic blockbuster to your budget, then settle for brief sightseeing excursions near home. Stay within 100 miles, take a picnic lunch, and head for a new spot each time. It will probably take several years to see your entire area, but it will be an enriching experience. Happy holidays!

# ELEVEN
# LEFT ALONE
# AT SEVENTY-FIVE

Often the years pass so rapidly that even those of more than threescore and ten years are surprised and shocked at the death of a loved one or spouse. If one is not emotionally and spiritually prepared for the loss, the consequences can be devastating. Emotional breakdowns, financial setbacks, and even physical problems may occur because of the shocks involved.

The Lord has indicated in his Word that we are to be good stewards. But this involves much more than stewardship of money alone. It also includes time and talent, as well as physical, emotional, and spiritual strength and abilities.

If one has been a careful steward of all his God-given resources, he can more easily cope with the homegoing of a mate or other loved one. The Lord has said, "I will never leave thee nor forsake thee," and David adds, in Psalm 139:18, 19, that God's thoughts toward us (his children) are precious and more numerous than the sand. In response to his heavenly Father's absolute concern, David exclaims in the same psalm, "When I awake, I am still with thee" (v. 19). God is interested in the total man, not just his spiritual needs. Knowing that the Lord loves us and is anxious to supply every need, we can entrust Christian loved ones to his care and keeping with confidence. At the same time, we can be assured of his loving concern for our own lives and future.

Being an active participant in a local Bible-believing church, attending the services regularly, enjoying fellowship with believers in an adult Sunday school class, missionary circle, or men's fellowship group, and serving wherever one can while actively seeking to witness for Christ is the best way to make this difficult transition a success-ful one. One frequently hears an aged widow or widower say, "But I don't really feel like being around other people." Yet this is exactly what is needed at a time like this—fellowship, fellowship, and more fellowship, not lonely, solitary hours.

All of this may seem quite rudimentary and not at all earth-shaking, but it is the best way to endure the shock of the loss of a loved one. It will not only take you through the "valley of the shadow" with blessing but will likewise make you a blessing to others. God's will is that we continue to produce fruit in old age (Psalm 92:14). This is only possible if you are a Spirit-controlled believ-er at any age. When physical strength wanes, the personal work of the Spirit becomes just that much more important.

When a loved one goes home to be with the Lord, it is of prime importance that the surviving spouse be financially solvent and in good spiritual, emotional, and physical health. The local church and Christian friends can furnish tremendous support.

Another way to avoid loneliness is to witness regularly for Christ and to keep active socially. An interest in the souls and welfare of others prevents us from thinking selfishly and from drowning in self-pity.

Our hobbies and interests can also be of great value in keeping us occupied and happy. After losing his wife at eighty, one man took over her "job" of supplying the church with flowers every Sunday. He continued to work in his garden and greenhouse, as well as the church, until the Lord took him home too.

Another saint who lost a beloved husband remained active in her local church and used extra time for door-to-door calling and our Televangelism ministry. She is radiant and blessed because she is always sharing her faith with others.

One dear brother, who became a widower at seventy-five, volunteered to drive the new pastor around on his house calls until he became familiar with the streets and neighborhoods of the entire town.

All of these have adapted well because they were in good spiritual shape when the shock of losing a loved one came. I personally believe, after being in the ministry for over twenty years, that this can be true of any born-again Christian who is walking with his Savior. He does not have to fall apart at the seams, give up, or abide in loneliness. Truly God can be "our refuge and our strength" and will enable us "to do all things through Christ" (see Psalm 46:1 and Philippians 4:13). May this be your portion and blessing as you put God to the test and find him sufficient for your every need.

Please remember, dear friend, that believers in Christ will meet again. The amazing and wonderful thing is that we will "be like him; for we shall see him as he is" (1 John 3:2). If this is your hope, then retirement, death, and separation are only temporary, transient phenomena which will soon pass away, after which we will join our Savior and loved ones forever.

Those who practice godliness will abide forever, and all their needs will be met by a loving God. Being left alone at seventy-five is not easy, but God can calm your heart and continue to make you a blessing to others.

# TWELVE
# GOD'S PROMISES
# TO THE AGING

". . . I will never leave thee, nor forsake thee"
(Hebrews 13:5).

In the last analysis, when our estates are
planned and children cared for, we must trust
the Lord implicitly to provide for us and to
sustain us spiritually, mentally, and physically all
the way through to glory. The Old Testament
speaks of trusting God in Psalms 56:3, 22:8 and
2:12, as well as in 149 other places. The text is
literally saying "roll your burdens on the Lord."
For you see, there are burdens and trials in life
that we cannot bear alone. We must bear the
burdens of others (Galatians 6:2), which they may
be unable to face without our support. We may
have to endure a personal burden, as did the
Apostle Paul, which we cannot carry alone and
which God does not choose to remove. This is the
type of burden which one must finally roll upon
the Lord.

Because he loves his children, God promises to
watch over them and care for them. The psalmist

puts this beautifully in Psalm 139:4–6, "For there is not a word in my tongue, but, lo, O Lord, thou knowest it altogether. Thou hast beset me behind and before, and laid thine hand upon me. Such knowledge is too wonderful for me; it is high, I cannot attain unto it." Again in verses 17, 18 the psalmist reminds us of God's love and concern by saying, "How precious also are thy thoughts unto me, O God! how great is the sum of them! If I should count them, they are more in number than the sand: when I awake, I am still with thee." He knows all about us because he sees the heart. He loves us so much that his thoughts are constantly upon us. In Psalm 92:14, God says that we "shall bring forth fruit in old age" and "shall be fat and flourishing [spiritually]." With all of these promises and more, why shouldn't we trust God to provide for every need and sustain us, no matter what our burden?

One of my aunts, a fine Christian lady, developed rheumatoid arthritis in her late fifties. During the next twenty years she suffered much pain, went through major surgery several times, and spent the last nine or ten years of her life in a nursing home. In spite of this, she was one of the most cheerful people I have ever met, always ready with a smile and word of cheer for others. Truly the Lord was her light and salvation, and she was filled with his Spirit. Rather than trying to bear her own burdens or shifting them to her loved ones' shoulders, she learned to cast her burdens on the Lord. This comes about by walking with the Lord and praying in faith through the years. One day I asked my cousin how her mother could take the pain and be so genial. She replied, "Because she's a fine Christian, that's why." That was the only possible answer.

Another woman was informed by her doctor at sixty-two that she had only a short time to live and that she should get her affairs in order. This shock caused her to turn to Christ. For over twenty years she stayed in her own home, renting out rooms and managing to survive without welfare on a very meager income. Even a city sewer assessment failed to daunt her. When borrowed money came due, she told the holder of the note (who happened to be her lawyer) that she would need more time to pay off the principal. He simply reached across the desk, picked up the note, wrote on it "paid in full," and with a smile handed it back.

She came home bubbling over with joy, for her Lord had again supplied her need. I watched her live by faith for twenty-two years, and she died (with no debts) in 1970 at the age of eighty-four. By the way, her non-Christian doctor died at sixty-three or sixty-four, leaving his wife in dire straits even though he had made tens of thousands of dollars per year for many years. What made the difference? Quite simply, God takes care of his own.

In old age, our biggest problem is usually taking God at his word and trusting him with everything. "The more we trust, the better we fare" is as much a truism today as when first spoken.

As you grow older, remember your problems are not yours alone. Millions around you face the same troubles, and those who have gone before have endured them too. Yes, we are living longer today, with better health and resources to cope with our problems, but we must still learn to adapt and trust God implicitly, as must every generation. As you learn to trust, ask, and receive, God will answer by increasing your faith and outreach, making you a fruitful blessing in old age.

# THIRTEEN
# CHILDREN'S
# MARITAL PROBLEMS

While calling one evening, I stopped at a home where I was greeted by Grandmother. She thought I was from the Sunday school and asked if I wanted "his," "hers," or "our" children. Her daughter had been divorced and remarried, and so had her son-in-law. Both of them had children by their first marriages and also by the present union. Because Grandmother had lived in another part of the country, she had not known her daughter's children when they were small, nor, of course, her new son-in-law's children. Therefore, the present crop of little ones were "ours." One may laugh at this bit of polite sarcasm, but all too often, it is the way of life in our generation.

Perhaps the Law #7 of the aged should be: *Try diligently to keep yourself from being judge and jury in your adult children's lives.* I have seen children forsake their parents because the parents fought with their children's spouses. I have also seen families split up because grandparents wanted to rear their grandchildren.

Neither you nor your children will be happy if you try to impose all of your values on them and their offspring. You had eighteen years in which to build your values and life style into your children. Now pray for them and be supportive, but let them lead their own lives, as difficult as it may be sometimes. They may not always please you, but you'll be happier in the long run, and you'll be closer to them and more able to help if they need you.

Remember what I said earlier in this book about children who want to run their parents' lives and impose their value systems on them in old age? Well, it can work much the same way in reverse! Once your children have married and made their own home, they are to "cleave" to each other (Genesis 2:24; Matthew 19:5). In addition, they are to leave father and mother and establish their own home. They will be mature and independent if you have done your job well, but you'll see plenty of them when they need you, or lack assurance or security. They may not approach you from that point of reference, but you will hear from them nevertheless. In fact, some of the most mature and independent young people are always looking for "excuses" to see Mom and Dad because such a good relationship and rapport have been established. There can be a wonderful feeling of family unity, without running one another's lives. This is called Christian maturity.

I like what one Christian mother told her daughter who had been married for several months to a wonderful boy. Upset because business had taken him out of town for a few days, the daughter wanted to leave him and come home to Mama. She felt that he must not really love her anymore, and was feeling very sorry for herself.

Mother simply told her, "First, Honey, you married Jim and he is your husband; second, you took him for better or for worse; and third, since he is your husband, you'll have to go to him and talk this out. Please remember to go to the Lord first, and then bear in mind that Jim's house is now your home. The problem is yours and his, and you will not be coming home to live with us. Your father and I will pray for you and give sought-after advice, but we will not try to run your home, just as we can't allow you to run ours."

Twenty years later this "young couple" is still happily married and laughs about that call. Mom used her head and considered Jim as much a part of her family as her own daughter. Because she was supportive while refusing to interfere in their marriage, Jim loved her for it.

As I said previously, these principles work both ways and are timeless. They are certainly not pertinent only for a particular age or group. With proper communication, there ought to be no generation gap in mature Christian homes. Jim's in-laws had raised their daughter as a Christian and had instilled certain principles in her heart that later solved the "domestic crisis."

Contrast this with parents who allowed their daughter to leave her husband of twelve years when he was away in service and she was lonely and feeling sorry for herself. When she went home to Mom and Daddy, they took her in, babied her, and broke up her marriage. She never recovered. In fact, she became an alcoholic. She really loved her husband but wasn't mature enough to handle the immediate problem without Mom and Dad.

This young lady, who had a great deal of talent, remained an alcoholic for over thirty years until her father and mother both died. Then she accepted responsibility and put her life together. No longer an alcoholic, she is a happy, active individual. But what a price to pay for parental interference! If her parents had insisted that she return to her husband, years of heartache for everyone could have been avoided.

If any group of people need to be free and unshackled, it is retired couples who have worked a lifetime in order to gain enough independence to do many things they couldn't afford or didn't have time to do before retirement.

Therefore, Law #7 of the aged should be adhered to as scrupulously as possible. *Try diligently to keep yourself from being judge and jury in your adult children's lives.*

# FOURTEEN
# THE CHURCH'S RESPONSIBILITY TO THE AGED

We hear a great deal in this generation about our responsibility to our church and its mission, but very little concerning the church's responsibility to its elderly members. Just what should the local church be doing for its older, retired members? What does it owe to them? We read in James 1:27, "Pure religion and undefiled before God and the Father is this, To visit the fatherless and widows in their affliction, and to keep himself unspotted from the world."

Dorcas is known in Acts 9 as a woman "full of good works and almsdeeds." The giving of alms was important in that day because there was no welfare, Social Security, or food stamps. God devised a plan for the ancient Hebrews, inaugurated through Moses, to care for aged parents. First, children were to honor or reverence their parents, to respect them, listen to them, and cause them to have joy. Second, they were not to rob or abuse their parents financially.

The Old Testament says little about caring for

poor family members beyond this. God expected
relatives to attend to such matters. References are
made, however, concerning the poor stranger
and his care. Because Israelites were instructed by
God to raise up heirs to carry on the family
name, they were assured of occupants for the
family land, which was passed on in perpetuity.
Thus the family unit was kept intact, and there
were always family members on the land to care
for needy relatives. Even in the case of Ruth, a
foreign relative by marriage, Boaz, a kinsman,
showed kindness and instructed his harvesters to
be generous with her.

The Bible and Jewish tradition tell us much
about care of the poor in general. Whatever the
harvesters dropped in the fields was not to be
picked up, but remained for the poor so they
would not starve. Furthermore, the corners of the
fields were not cut square but rounded off, leaving some grain and crops for the poor. If clothes
or blankets were given as a pledge for a debt, the
impoverished were even allowed to have them
back at night to keep from being cold.

The Jews gave liberally to care for the poor.
They often rendered a tithe or 10 percent for the
poor in addition to their tithe to the synagogue
and 20 percent in tax to the Roman government.
When the Temple was built in Jerusalem, many
faithful Jews donated another 10 percent for the
Temple care, the priests, and the poor in Jerusalem. It was also commonplace to see alms being
given to the afflicted at the Temple gate and at
places like Hezekiah's Pool.

The Pharisees often contributed additional

amounts in public to the poor, sick, and afflicted as a show of piety. The faithful Jews who had compassion would, therefore, give about 30 percent of their income in tithes, offerings, and love gifts besides paying 20 percent in taxes. It's interesting to note that the Pharisees, who encouraged and practiced such beneficence, were among the wealthiest people in Israel, showing that God honored their generosity.

In New Testament times with more urbanized living, there were many poor who had no family or visible means of support. This, of course, became a great problem for the New Testament churches, and God gave instruction concerning the poor Christian widow who was without family or relatives to care for her.

"But if any widow have children or nephews [descendants or relatives], let them learn first to show piety [or godliness] at home, and to requite [meet the needs of] their parents: for that is good and acceptable before God" (1 Timothy 5:4). We should also listen to the Lord's admonition in 1 Timothy 5:8, "But if any provide not for his own, and specially for those of his own house, he hath denied the faith, and is worse than an infidel."

Remember in all of this, that a biblical "chain of command" exists. We are to be subject to God first, then to our parents, to those in spiritual authority over us in the local church, and then in varying degrees to our teachers or employers, and so on. As we consider our money, we are first to give God his tithe and our offerings; then we are to care for our immediate family. If our aged parents have need, we are to honor them and supply their needs as we are able to do so.

God's Word then goes a step further concerning those who have no family to care for them. It defines responsibility in 1 Timothy 5:9, 10 by saying, "Let not a widow be taken into the number [church care] under threescore [60] years old, having been the wife of one man, well reported of for good works; if she have relieved the afflicted, if she have diligently followed every good work."

God set up the pattern, establishing certain conditions and restrictions. Only those who were over sixty, without family and support, who had faithfully raised their children, been hospitable, helped others, and maintained an excellent report for doing good were to be supported by the church. This seems to relieve the church of any major concern for the careless, unloving, unspiritual Christian. Furthermore, 1 Timothy 5:16 indicates that if any widow has relatives, they, not the church, are to care for her. This, of course, speaks directly of food, clothing, shelter, and such temporal needs. With our welfare system today, Social Security supplements, Medicare and Medicaid, etc., very few seniors are completely destitute, but our responsibility is still there when needs are present.

The pattern shown in God's Word, then, is that the church should only care for widows who have no family to help them. This establishes a minimum responsibility, but doing more is certainly not wrong. Witness Dorcas in Acts 9 as an exam-

ple of good works, and Cornelius as a pattern for
almsgiving in Acts 10:31.

Beyond physical needs lie spiritual and emotional needs. Just what is the responsibility of the
church in these areas that are not so well de-
fined? A total ministry by the church to the total
man or woman, regardless of his or her age, is
taught in God's Word. Yet as I have moved
across this country, taking note of scores of
churches, serving on the pastoral staff in six
churches, and working in two others as a layman,
I have realized that most are not meeting the
spiritual and emotional needs of our elderly
Christians.

Why is this the case? In many instances we
have not taught our young people respect for age
as the Bible admonishes. In addition, we have not
disciplined their lives, nor taught them to serve
others. Selfish people only serve themselves, while
spiritual, outgoing, caring, soul-winning people
live to meet the needs of others, as did Christ our
example, servant, and Lord! These spiritual souls
cultivate a lifetime of generosity as a means of
preparing for service in later years and of pleas-
ing the Lord.

Just how can we, individually and as a local
body, meet our responsibility to the elderly in the
flock? By remembering that they may be older,
but inside they are no different than you or me.
They need to be useful and serving. When needs
arise, they need to be ministered to just as with
anyone else—not by the elderly alone, but also by
the young.

Our senior youth pastor has made a habit of

holding a Christmas tea for our Live Wires spon-
sored by the senior high young people, who
provide a handmade present for every senior. In
addition, a young person sits next to each oldster
and introduces him or her to the entire group.
Our young people also hold periodic workdays
and are available to do menial tasks for *free*
around the house, yard, or apartment as a gesture of love and concern. They occasionally visit
our shut-ins and sing carols and hymns to them
just to demonstrate their love for the older saints.
In return, they inform the elderly of prayer
requests and needs, and ask for their prayers.

Even our ten-year-old boys in Boys Brigade
have held workdays at the homes of shut-ins.
They have shown that no generation gap exists
among dedicated Christians. After one such
workday, a ninety-two-year-old shut-in, with tears
in her eyes, confessed that she hadn't believed
that any ten-year-old youngster could care about
an old lady like her. That day did all of them,
both young and old, a great deal of good spiritually and emotionally.

Our church deaconesses minister extensively to
shut-ins and the aged. The ladies visit them,
maintain a prayer chain for emergency health
needs and other burdens, aid them with food and
transportation to church and doctors, take flowers
to them, and call on the phone to reassure and
help them. This, along with our Deacons' Shep-
herding program, provides each of our elderly
with personal contacts within the church family.
Each deacon is assigned a number of members to
whom he ministers and gives support in time of

need. This, of course, includes the elderly and shut-ins. If folks are absent two Sundays, the church sends a personal letter of inquiry. After two more Sundays of absence, a deacon is given the name for a follow-up visit.

Our adult Sunday school classes endeavor to keep track of their members, visiting and encouraging them as needed. The Sunday school also maintains a roll and seeks to follow up on all absentees.

The elderly, like those of us who are younger, can be helped by people to whom they relate, regardless of age. In direct personal counseling, however, the experience of aged people ministering to younger people is often most beneficial because their experience undergirds their understanding of what the younger person is going through. The older deacon and deaconess can often successfully counsel the elderly and identify more readily with them.

# FIFTEEN
# CHRISTIAN CHILDREN'S RESPONSIBILITY TO THEIR PARENTS

From the dawn of creation, God has ordained that family members should care for each other's needs and that needy elderly should be attended to by their own children. In our generation, we have sought to delegate this to the state or whoever else would accept the burden. However, this cannot set aside God's plan or absolve us from our responsibilities.

The Bible commands in Exodus 20:12, "Honor thy father and thy mother: that thy days may be long upon the land which the Lord thy God giveth thee." Leviticus 19:3 tells us to fear or reverence our fathers. In Leviticus 19:32, the Israelites were to rise or stand in respect before the hoary or gray head and to honor the face of the elderly man. Proverbs enjoins us to heed a father's instruction and not to forsake a mother's training (see Proverbs 1:8; 4:1; 6:20; 13:1; and 15:5).

We are, furthermore, not to waste our father

(reducing him to poverty) or chase away our mother; we must not despise our mother when she is old (Proverbs 23:22). In fact, the one robbing his father or mother is considered by God as the companion of a destroyer. In addition, Proverbs 29:7 says, "The righteous considereth the cause of the poor." We are exhorted neither to curse our parents nor to mock them (Proverbs 30:11, 17). If any Israelite refused to obey his father or mother and remained stubborn and rebellious, a glutton and drunkard, he was to be stoned (Deuteronomy 21:18–21).

According to the New Testament, believers are not to designate funds for charity to the neglect of their father or mother. Such an action makes God's Word "of none effect through tradition" (Mark 7:11–13). First Timothy 5:8 says, "But if any provide not for his own, and specially for those of his own house, he hath denied the faith, and is worse than an infidel."

The biblical pattern is very clear: children care for their own parents' needs and thus honor them before the Lord. In fact, 1 Timothy 5:4 says that widows having children or descendants are to be cared for by them. This shows true piety or spirituality; it is good and acceptable before God. The phrase "to requite their parents" literally means "to give off from one's self" or to discharge a burden, like a debt, as a matter of family honor. It covers any living relatives, and puts the burden of supporting one's father, mother, grandfather, or grandmother directly in the hands of the children and grandchildren.

Good wishes are not enough. Honoring one's

parents continues throughout life and includes the financial realm. One cannot really honor one's parents and yet allow them to go without the necessities of life. The immediate family, of course, should come first, but this does not do away with our responsibility to help care for Mom's and Dad's needs.

In our generation, most general and emergency needs are cared for by pensions, Social Security, savings, the state, and insurance. In the event of some special emergency needs, how much more honoring to the Lord it would be if children offer to help. Rather than merely saying, "We'll help you when you're broke" and neglecting the need altogether, each family member could donate a little each month until the need was met.

No one wants to be destitute, especially at seventy-five or eighty years of age. It would be so much more beneficial for children to send twenty or twenty-five dollars a month *before* their parents are at the bottom of the barrel. It would bring joy, lift the burden, help spiritually and emotionally, and fulfill Galatians 6:2 and Ephesians 6:2. This is one way of showing honor to one's parents.

We who are still working and earning do not realize what it is like to face old age without adequate income because of inflation or illness, or to face depleted reserves with no way to replenish them. This simply panics many people. It's easy to say "Trust the Lord and don't worry," but much more difficult to do it when old age, ill health, and senility begin to affect the body and mind. Thus, anything we can do to take pressures and disturbing problems from our parents' shoulders will help them—and us—in the long run.

The occasional phone call, letter, special visit, or invitation to dinner can often cheer the lonely heart, relax tensions, and provide a spiritual lift because someone cares. Nothing deadens Dad's and Mom's spirits quicker than careless children who don't communicate or try to understand and help with problems. They may sometimes seem a little odd, stubborn, and set in their ways, but after a lifetime of wear and tear, we'll all be much like them. Let's try to understand now so that we'll be better equipped when we get there!

I think of one dear couple who provided a good home for their children and as much of an education as was possible during the 1930s. One son was killed in the war; the other son moved away and never returned. It broke the parents' hearts because the one they loved most ignored them except for an occasional letter or card. He did not honor his parents.

Another couple worked hard, sent their only son through college, and made sure he was well established in life. After Dad died, the son and his wife seldom if ever darkened Mom's door. Though they lived nearby, they only invited her over for dinner on Thanksgiving and Christmas, and then only for a few hours.

When Mom dies, guess who will be the first in line to get her home and assets? That's right, her son and his wife get everything! The mother is dying with a broken heart because she knows that her son doesn't really care about her. I've often thought how wonderful it would have been if her son had only picked her up and taken her for a ride occasionally, or even let her sit in the car while he fished nearby. At least her emotional needs would have been met, and it would have cost him so little in time and money to be such a big blessing.

Some years ago, a bachelor son retired from the Merchant Marines and came back home. His mother was in a nursing facility already, but he faithfully visited her every week and took her for rides past the old house and neighborhood. This really *made her week* and kept her perfectly content, though she was confined to a wheelchair all of the time. Why? Because she knew that her son really loved her, and so everything was well in her world. Oh yes, she had pain from arthritis and other ills (she was in her nineties), but she tolerated them with God's help because her soul was happy and filled with joy.

Many elderly people have lived an extra five or ten years with comparatively good health simply because they were loved and wanted. Love and caring are free. Why not use them to God's glory and someone else's blessing?

Simply put, show reverence, love, and honor to your parents in a meaningful way. Pensions, Social Security, stocks, bonds, and the state may provide financial security, but human contact can give peace, joy, and emotional and spiritual stability.

One elderly lady stayed alternately with three daughters. She generally spent the winters with two daughters in California and the summers with her daughter in the Midwest. When her strength failed, the daughter in the Midwest cared for her until she died. She left that daughter and son-in-law her home because of their many years of free, loving care. The cash and bonds were divided equally among the three daughters. Everyone was satisfied, the three sisters remained close in their relationship, and God's Word was honored. One daughter passed away at seventy-four, one is now seventy-three, and the other is seventy-seven. Because they honored their mother, God gave them length of days and family blessing. Following God's principles always brings fulfillment and blessing.

One of the easiest favors to bestow on older people, and yet one of the most neglected, is to visit them regularly. Years ago when I was a boy, it was an ordinary thing for children to visit Grandmother and Grandfather or some other relatives on a Sunday afternoon. Many times the visits were purely social, or to verify that the "old folks" were all right, but they really met a need and brought joy to the hearts of the elderly.

When visiting relatives at ten or twelve years of age, I can remember being asked to go to an aged relative's room. I would knock on the door, be invited in, say hello, and pass the time of day, answering questions and engaging in conversation just because it was expected of young folks in our family. This meant very little to me then, but I can readily see the value of it now. In fact, one aged relative lived to be almost 100 years old and was on her feet and mentally alert almost until the end. I attribute much of it to the love, respect, tranquility, and tender care that she received.

Another great blessing to older people, especially when they are faithful Christians, is to have loved ones share spiritual experiences and the Word of God with them. Just having a son or daughter, grandson or granddaughter stop by and read from God's Word and pray will lift the spirits of the elderly and make their entire week. Usually the one who goes to *minister* comes away having been *ministered to*, without realizing it.

One of the best ways to keep the elderly healthy and happy is to take them shopping, or to invite them over for dinner occasionally. It gives them something to look forward to and shortens the monotonous, colorless hours. It is a simple gesture and doesn't cost a lot, but it can pay rich dividends: (1) the children are obeying God's Word; (2) God promises length of days for this obedience; and (3) keeping one's parents spiritually and emotionally happy will generally result in better physical health and thus less cost, difficulty, and days spent in nursing homes and hospitals. This may sound a little selfish, but it's really just good, common sense. We can never outdo God's generosity when we are obedient to his Word. Many elderly people spend a great deal of their assets for psychiatric counseling when some loving care and concern would have prevented many of their emotional and physical problems.

It is important to minister to the whole person physically, mentally, and spiritually. It is also necessary to follow God's program, plan, and standards if we are to enjoy a happy, harmonious family life and relationship. Helping our elderly progress into a more fruitful, happy retirement is within the grasp of every Christian family, but we have to work at it and plan for it like anything else. God promises to bless us in it and to enrich our lives as we bring blessing to one another. For you see, God's plan in his "chain of command" is that children love and honor their parents, obey them, and meet their needs when they can no longer care for themselves. This may sound outmoded, but in reality it's the biblical plan.

As we honor our parents in their later years and show them proper respect, God will bless us with peace in our heart and length of days upon the land which he has given us, according to his promise in Exodus 20:12. In addition, God seems to grant to us in old age a measure of what we have given to our loving parents. May this also encourage each of us to show concern and respect for our parents so that their golden years *and ours* may be blessed and more fruitful.

# SIXTEEN
# BECOMING FRIENDS THROUGH THE YEARS

It has been said that a friend is someone who knows all about you and still loves you! In most cases, children love their parents and want God's best for them, but helping them achieve this in their late years may seem difficult. We must, however, understand that Mom and Dad, advanced in years and enduring a changing (and often pain-wracked) body, are not always going to be on top of the world. They may have an inner peace and satisfaction, but physical pain may take the joy out of living and even bring about a complaint or two.

At this stage in life, it is most helpful to them if we can be supportive and encouraging. Those who have drawn close to their parents, and have allowed them to become friends and important companions, are able to cope with old age and senility during later years. Why? Because they have tried to understand and have developed a good relationship with Mom and Dad.

I have seen a son-in-law lovingly carry his wife's

mother around the house and even to the car
and doctor's office with a smile. In some cases
Mom or Dad feel closer to a son-in-law or
daughter-in-law because they have built up a solid
rapport. How did this come about? By genuine
interest in each other's problems and needs.

An elderly parent often thanked her daughter-
in-law for her loving care and then mentioned
that she was praying for *her* needs as well.
Friendship will inevitably blossom when someone
loves you, thanks you, and prays for you. Those
things just naturally build up our self-image.

Drawing closer to one's parents or in-laws in
later years is definitely a two-way street. It can be
repulsed or encouraged by either party. The best
way is simply to start. If your attitudes haven't
been right, wade right in and begin to sweeten
the relationship. You'll be surprised at how quickly Mom and Dad respond to a little loving care
and practical concern. Proverbs 15:5 puts it so
well by saying, "All the days of the afflicted are
evil: but he that is of a merry heart hath a
continual feast." If we make the heart cheerful,
the remaining burdens of the elderly will seem
minimal. Many of them have lived with pain for a
number of years. What they can't understand and
accept is neglect and lack of love.

Begin making friends with your parents or
aging relatives. Notice the startling difference in
their dispositions in a short time. In fact, the
extra bonus may just well be an improvement in
their physical well-being, because a merry heart
acts like medicine to the entire body.

A famous psychologist once wrote that in a

lifetime, the average person only has three to five close friends in whom he can really confide and pour out his heart. Most of us probably have fewer than three such persons with whom we really share our soul's deepest longings. It therefore becomes very important for us to develop that kind of rapport with a son or daughter as we grow older and lose our friends.

Some years ago, a mother who suffered from tuberculosis of the bone spent her last few months lying in a hammock instead of in bed in order to ease her pain. During those difficult months, she and her daughter had great fellowship in the Word and in prayer. This sick mother developed such a happy relationship with her daughter and son-in-law that she became a radiant Christian and blessed the hearts of all who came to see her and offer encouragement. Her cup was full to overflowing in spite of her pain and difficulty because she had love and security, and her emotional and spiritual needs were met in a wonderful way.

An elderly mother in her nineties lived with her daughter who, with her husband, enjoyed a wonderful relationship with the mother. In fact, the respect and honor shown by the son-in-law was profound, for he loved her greatly. They took Mother on vacations with them and treated her like a queen. I never heard a cross word among them, and I really marveled at their loving patience with a sick, elderly mother. This is certainly what the Lord meant by honoring one's parents so that our days might be long upon the land which he has given to us.

Admittedly, such relationships are not common, but they are the ideal and certainly will be blessed of God.

Some would probably ask at this point, "But how do I begin to develop this relationship when it has never before existed?" First, there must be a desire for it, and then positive steps must be taken to bring it about. Perhaps the best of all approaches would be to put Ephesians 4 and 5 into practice. This will establish a firm base for restoring poor relationships and prepare us for a good start toward building a vital friendship with our father or mother, son or daughter. Ephesians 4:30–32 and 5:18b–21 are particularly important. If each can see the love of Christ and a genuine Spirit-controlled life in the other as well as genuine concern for his or her welfare, friendly relationships will flourish.

The aging process, as we have seen, can be meaningful and rewarding if we apply God's principles to every area of life. With the experiences of life to guide us and God leading us, the elderly years can be the most meaningful of all.